THEN AND THERE SERIES
GENERAL EDITOR
MARJORIE REEVES M.A. PH.D.

A Border Woollen Town in the Industrial Revolution

Karen McKechnie

Illustrated from contemporary sources
Line drawings by Toni Goffe

LONGMAN

LONGMAN GROUP LIMITED
London

Associated companies, branches and representatives throughout the world

© Longman Group Ltd 1968

First published 1968
Fourth impression 1975

ISBN 0 582 20451 8

Printed in Hong Kong by Sheck Wah Tong Printing Press

To W.P.M.

ACKNOWLEDGEMENTS

My thanks for assistance and advice in the preparation of this book are due to a great
many people, but particularly to Dr J. G. Martindale and Mr T. A. Stillie of the Scottish
Woollen Technical College, Galashiels; and to Mr Ian Brown of Wilderburn Mill,
Galashiels. I am also indebted to the Manufacturers' Corporation of Galashiels for the
use of their Minutes; to Mrs S. D. Wheeler Carmichael for permission to reproduce
the picture of Skirling Fair.

Permission to reproduce other illustrations was given by the following: the National
Library of Scotland for pp. 14, 15, 20, 37, 41, 45, 47, 48, 52, 57, 58, 63, 70, 72, 81
and 83; Edinburgh Public Library for pp. 10 and 85; Selkirk Public Library for pp. 24,
27 and 30. *The Penny Wedding* on p. 26 is reproduced by gracious permission of H.M.
the Queen.

Contents

TO THE READER

When we buy a tweed suit or skirt, we are not surprised if we find a label which reads, 'Fine Woollens woven in Scotland,' and which tells us that the cloth was made in Hawick or Jedburgh, in Peebles or Galashiels; for Scottish woollens are famous all over the world and are a valuable export. But it is only just over a hundred years since the name 'tweed' was first used to describe a cloth which was soon to become fashionable; and it is less than two hundred years since 'Galashiels Greys' were admitted to be poor stuff compared with English cloth.

We are going to look at the woollen industry in the Scottish Borders at a very important time, just when the new machines invented by John Kay, James Hargreaves and others in England were beginning to be used in Scotland; and we shall look mainly at one town, Galashiels, because it had some very enterprising manufacturers at the start of the nineteenth century and because it was closely associated with one of Scotland's most famous men, Sir Walter Scott, who not only lived and wrote at Abbotsford, but was Sheriff of Selkirkshire for many years and was one of the earliest wearers of the new tweeds.

But it was not Sir Walter Scott who took the steps which started the Galashiels woollen trade on the path to prosperity. It was men like George Mercer, who came to the village some-time in the 1770s, and built the first factory in Scotland which used water-power to produce yarn for weaving. Then there was Richard Lees, who was one of the earliest to try out John Kay's flying shuttle in the village. There were also the Thom-sons, David and William, who brought spinning mules to the village in 1814, and the Sandersons, whose eldest member, Alexander, was not only a woollen manufacturer but also, for some years, a farmer at Newcastleton, a few miles from the Border.

These were some of the men who were the pioneers in bring-ing the new machines to Galashiels and so turning it into a factory town; but even they could not have done this without the help of a body called the Board of Trustees for Manufactures in Scotland which gave grants to manufacturers for buying new equipment, for making trips to England to learn how to use them, for new inventions or for improving buildings. We are rather apt to think that our century is bound to be ahead of the ones which went before it in everything to do with industry, so it is just as well that we should know that the idea of helping manufacturers to improve their businesses is not a new one at all.

Without the enterprise of the manufacturers and the help given by the Board of Trustees, there would have been no tweed trade as it is today.

Words printed *in italics* are explained in the Glossary (p. 93).

1 The Woollen Trade in Scotland

Woollen goods had been made in Scotland for a long time before tweeds were thought of, but mostly they had been of a poor, coarse quality, and the trade had not been a very thriving one. In fact, in 1681, the Scottish Parliament passed a law forbidding the import of linen, calico and cotton goods, and the aim of this was to encourage the manufacturers of woollens and linens by forcing people to wear clothes made from these yarns. Various factories were set up, including a large one which employed over two hundred workers at New Mills in Haddington, not far from Edinburgh.

But even with the encouragement which it had been given, the woollen trade did not prosper very greatly, and after the Act of Union of 1707 matters became worse because English cloth was not only of better quality but could be made and sold more cheaply to the Scots than their own woollens. All the same, coarse woollens continued to be made in quite a lot of places, and we know what some of these were from a list made in 1733.

If you look at the map on page 4, you will see that woollen goods were made here and there from the Borders to Aberdeen, but that most of the places are in the southern half of the country. Can you think of any reasons for this?

Another thing which you may have noticed is that all the goods sound rough and unattractive—except for Edinburgh's 'fine *shalloons*'. The other places were making the kind of goods which would be bought by ordinary folk for everyday use: cheap serges, which may have stood up well to hard wear but must have been very ugly; and stockings and blankets made from wool which had been treated with tar, and which

Aberdeen: Coarse, Tarred-Wool Serges and Stockings.

Edinburgh: Fine Shalloons.

Galashiels: 'Galashiels Greys'.

Hawick: Tarred-Wool Blankets, Etc.

Kilmarnock: Cheap Serges.

Kirkcudbright: Tarred-Wool Blankets, Etc.

Musselburgh: Cheap Goods.

Stirling: Cheap Serges, Etc.

Places Where Woollen Goods were Manufactured In 1733

Aberdeen

Stirling

Edinburgh
Musselburgh

Kilmarnock
Galashiels

Selkirk

Hawick

Kirkcudbright

was often coarse and hard to start with.

You might expect that such low-quality goods could only be sold in Scotland and that nobody else would buy them; but we know that Aberdeen sent some of its products to London for export to Holland, which also bought some serges from Kilmarnock. Some of the cheap goods in Musselburgh were even exported to the West Indies! So Scottish woollens were reaching some outside markets, but we must remember that the trade was very small. The population of Scotland in the middle of the eighteenth century was only about $1\frac{1}{2}$ million, and none of the woollen towns on the map, apart from Edinburgh and Aberdeen, numbered more than one or two thousand, so their production must have been very small and must have been mainly for local use. An export drive could hardly be expected from a county like Selkirkshire, where everything was carried on pack-horses, because the first wheeled cart in the area was not built much before 1730.

2 The Woollen Trade in the Borders

It is time to take a closer look at the Borders, now, and you will see that this map shows the main Border towns in the 1770s, that is about forty years later than the last map. If you compare it with a physical one of Scotland in your atlas, you will also see that almost all of these places stand in valleys surrounded by hill-masses.

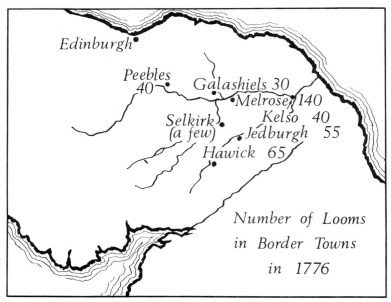

Edinburgh

Peebles 40

Galashiels 30

Melrose 140

Kelso 40

Selkirk (a few)

Jedburgh 55

Hawick 65

Number of Looms
in Border Towns
in 1776

Jedburgh : jobbing.
Kelso : woollen and linen cloth and carpets.
Melrose : woollen cloth.

Peebles : coarse woollens.
Selkirk : yarn manufacture and jobbing.
Galashiels : Galashiels Greys' and blankets.

Most of the land is unsuitable for arable farming, though some crops are grown in the valleys. But for the most part it is land for grazing cattle or sheep—particularly sheep, since they can survive hard weather conditions in the hills.

So, standing among the huge sheep-walks, the Border towns have for a long time been markets for livestock, meat and wool, and have slowly built up the one industry for which the raw material was right at hand—the making of cloth. And this is now such a valuable industry that it earns a great deal of money by exporting woollens abroad.

You can see that the only town with at all a large woollen industry in the 1770s was Melrose; all the others had quite a small number of looms, and even then, they mostly divided them between different sorts of goods. For instance, Hawick, with only sixty-five looms, was producing woollens and linen on fifty-one of them and carpets on the other fourteen, while Galashiels on its thirty looms made blankets as well as the coarse, narrow cloth known as 'Galashiels Greys'. So apart from Melrose, the Border towns must have been making woollen cloth on a rather small scale compared with some other towns at the same time, for example, Stirling with 160 looms, Ayr with a hundred, Alloa with 150 and Aberdeen with 240.

If you look again at the map, you will see that all these places in the Borders stand on rivers which are part of a hill and river system running more or less eastwards towards Berwick and the North Sea. In order to reach markets northwards (towards Edinburgh and Glasgow) or southwards (towards Newcastle or Carlisle), manufacturers had to carry their cloth on pack-horses across the lie of the land, and that meant up and down hills on roads which were so bad that carts were shaken to pieces on them in dry weather and stuck fast in pot-holes in wet weather. So the Border towns found it very difficult to reach outside markets, and until new machines improved the cloth which they had for sale and better roads were built to connect the Borders with the rest of Scotland and the north of England, the trade was bound to remain largely a local one. When our story begins, these changes were just starting to happen.

7

3 Galashiels about 1800

In 1803 William Wordsworth and his sister Dorothy made a tour through Scotland, and Dorothy kept a diary in which she wrote down her thoughts about the places which they visited. As they passed through the Borders, she wrote of Galashiels, 'A pretty place it has once been, but a manufactory has been established there; and a townish bustle and ugly stone houses are now taking place of the brown-roofed thatched cottages, of which a great number remain.' With that, she departed to more picturesque places: but we are going back to look at it as it was when she visited it.

The Edinburgh to Carlisle road of today follows the windings of Gala Water and runs through the busy town before swinging away along the Tweed Valley towards Selkirk; but in 1800, it by-passed Galashiels, and the road from the north was so bad that, when Gala Water was low, carters often found it easier to drive their waggons along the river-bed than to use the highway!

You can see from the map that the village consisted of one or two narrow streets lying between the river and the *mill-lade*. On either hand, green hillsides rose steeply, reaching 1400 feet at their highest point. Gala Hill—known locally as 'Gorgum'—was crowned by a dense, wild plantation, and, beneath it, at the south end of the village, were the wooded *policies* of Gala House, where the *lairds* of Gala, the Scott family, lived. At the entrance to the estate was the Old Town, with the parish church, the burial ground, the *Tolbooth* and the town Cross. Beyond the village the clear, brown stream flowed on to join the Tweed less than a mile away, and just across the Tweed was the '*Clarty* Hole', which the new Sheriff of Selkirkshire,

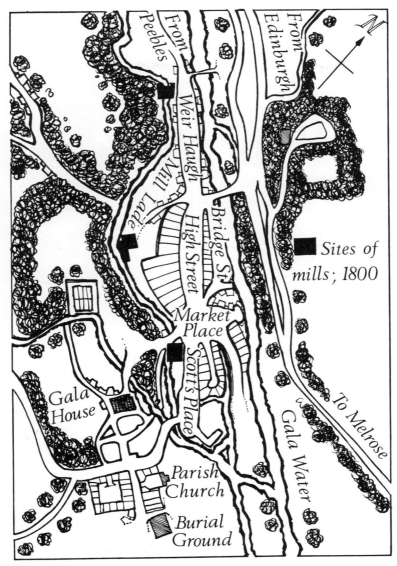

Labels visible on map: From Peebles; From Edinburgh; N; Weir Haugh; Mill Lade; High Street; Bridge St; Sites of mills; 1800; Market Place; Scott's Place; Gala House; Parish Church; Burial Ground; Gala Water; To Melrose

Galashiels about 1800

Abbotsford

Mr Walter Scott, was soon to turn into one of the most famous places in Scotland by building Abbotsford there.

Townish bustle there certainly is in Galashiels today, but we know, from calculations made in 1791 by Dr Douglas, the minister, that the population of the parish was then 914—and only about 600 of these lived in the village, the rest belonging to the country part of the parish. So it was probably not the number of people that Dorothy Wordsworth disliked so much as the manufactory.

All the same, Galashiels was growing, for the first time in forty years. There was a 'boom' in babies, as we can see when we read that there were 181 people from ten to twenty years old, but as many as 253 from nought to ten years old. Unless a great many of the youngest group died before growing up, there were likely to be more than usual marrying from 1800 onwards; and unless the looms of Galashiels could turn out more cloth, there was going to be less food in everybody's mouth.

Although we do not know just how many of the children did grow up, we do know something about the diseases which came to Galashiels. We hear no mention, at this time, of the dreaded cholera, but small-pox, measles and *chincough* returned to the parish again and again. However, inoculation for small-pox was starting to gain ground, and, when an epidemic came, as many as half of the children escaped infection, and very few died from it. (The conditions in which the inoculations were done were so bad that they were quite enough to have caused infections in themselves!) Mild fevers were frequent, and dysentery would sometimes sweep through the village, as was to be expected where there was no water-borne sanitation; but, oddly enough, the cause of the greatest number of deaths was said to be the sheer hardness of the work on top of poor diet and lack of cleanliness.

Dirt there certainly was: in backyards, steaming *middens* bred flies and fouled the air with their stench, while their seepage poisoned the wells from which the women drew drinking water. Even if the water had not been polluted, people would still have found it difficult to keep clean when every drop had to be pumped and carried indoors and then heated over an open fire.

Hours of work, too, were long for everybody. Children of eight or nine were often at work for up to eleven hours per day; the men in the mills worked at least as long; and, although weavers and spinners, in their homes, could knock off when it suited them, the fact was that, when there was yarn to be spun or cloth to be woven, they toiled on as long as the daylight lasted, and then by tallow candle, to earn a few pence more. They could not afford leisure, at an average wage of 1s 7d per day; nor could they afford to retire. Work was with them until they took to their beds for the last time, and even as they lay dying in the *close-bed* in the kitchen they could not escape from the clatter of the loom.

Diet, of course, meant porridge at least once a day! Porridge with milk began the day, and quite often ended it too, because milk and meal were among the cheapest foods which could be bought. Dinner might consist of some cheap cut of meat boiled with potatoes and onions; but meat was not always plentiful, and herrings, at ninepence the dozen, or Tweed salmon, at $1\frac{1}{2}$d per pound 'when it was in poor condition' might be eaten instead. Vegetables, apart from turnips, were hardly used at all, and fruit was not grown for sale, though back gardens might have a few stunted apple trees from which some sour green fruit could be picked. Oatmeal bannocks were eaten much as we eat bread, and, spread with butter or cheese, no doubt filled stomachs well enough. But it was a monotonous diet, and one on which it must have been hard to do a long day's work.

If you take a look at the map now, you can see that Dorothy Wordsworth was wrong on one point. There were at least three 'manufactories' at this time, not one. When you think of the word factory you probably imagine a tall, grimy building with a chimney pouring out black smoke. But the mills of Galashiels were not like that in 1800. Wilderhaugh Mill was sixty-five feet long by twenty-seven feet wide, with side walls sixteen feet high; and Mid Mill was the same height, but forty feet long and twenty-nine feet wide. So they were really no larger than one shop in a modern factory, and they could not have been more than two storeys tall. (As a matter of fact, the first really tall mill, one of four storeys, was not built until 1829.) And there was no question of smoky chimneys, because the mill machinery was driven by water-power. As you can see from the map, the mills stood beside the mill-lade, and their water-wheels, as much as 18 feet in diameter and ten feet wide, were driven by it and passed on their power through shafts and cogs to the machines. Not until 1831 was steam-power used, when a twenty-five horse-power engine was installed in one of the mills, and even then, the steam age did not make Galashiels a dirty industrial town like so many in the north of England and the Midlands.

In 1800, the mills only employed about fifty men and boys, but, from lists made at that time, we can work out roughly how many people were working at other jobs. There were:

about 43 weavers

about 240 full-time spinners

13 clothiers, who organized the woollen industry inside and

outside the mills

10 tanners, working at 2 tanneries

5 shoemakers

9 tailors

3 blacksmiths

17 *wrights,* some working as jobbing house-carpenters, some as wheelwrights for the mills, and some making and repairing waggons and farm-tools

3 bakers

2 candlemakers and

15 licensed houses.

'The number of shopkeepers cannot be easily ascertained,' adds Dr Douglas, who made up the list, 'as almost everybody buys and sells or barters'. His list is not quite complete, even so, because we know that there were also two masons in the village.

If you made a list of the ways in which people are employed in your neighbourhood today, it would look very different from Dr Douglas's; but if you keep in mind that a place like Galashiels had to supply most of its day-to-day needs, and that very few people had the leisure to enjoy the kind of amusements which we take for granted, you will probably begin to see why your list and his could not be the same; and you might try to see how you would change yours if you had to make almost everything for yourself instead of bringing much of it in, ready-made, from other places.

The narrow streets of Galashiels must have been full of interesting sights and sounds for the children who climbed the slope to the Burgh school in the Old Town. If they dawdled on the way, as they passed the bakehouses with their sweet, fermenting smell of new bread, nobody would blame them, except Mr Fyshe, the *dominie,* with his ever-ready *tawse.* Then, a horse might be being shod, and a boy could not be expected to tear himself away from the low door of the smithy until the glowing horseshoe had been beaten out in a shower of sparks on the anvil and clapped with an acrid sizzle on to the great hoof, and the nails hammered home with a metallic clink.

From cottage after cottage came the clattering of looms in the dark kitchens. Sometimes a woman would sit by the door at her spinning wheel, talking to a neighbour. Further on, there would be a *souter* at his last, stitching and hammering at heavy farm-boots; and a tailor might be sitting in his window, his needle flashing silently in and out of the cloth which he was making into a coat or a dress.

There might even be a couple of weavers passing the time in chatting until the next piece of work came along, and, rather surprisingly to our way of thinking, knitting as they talked!

Away above all the townish bustle, the laird of Gala could look down over his *barony* from the grounds of Gala House; but, for the time being, he left that to his mother—for the laird, John Scott, being only ten years old, had more interesting things to do, such as birds-nesting and riding and fishing. Yet all that went on in Galashiels was his business, for it was what was called a *burgh of barony*. There were various kinds of burghs in Scotland. Some of them, the royal burghs, had for a long time been represented in the Scottish Parliament and owned important privileges, such as the right to hold markets; or the *monopoly* of making some goods, like salt, for example; or the

A musical Souter

Working a stocking

right to collect their own taxes and send them to the king, instead of having his tax-collectors prying into everything. But the Scottish kings sometimes granted land, including a village or town, to a particular family as their barony, and in that case they would run it very much like a private estate, since all the townspeople were their tenants and owed certain dues to them. There would be no burgh council: instead, there would be an official called the *baron-bailie*, who was appointed by the laird and could be removed only by him. He was responsible for keeping order in the burgh, and he did this with the help of a constable of the watch. In past times, a baronial court had been held by the laird for punishing people who had committed small offences, such as brawling, petty thieving and so on; but in 1800 it was nearly a hundred years since the court had been held and the baron-bailie used to deal as best he could with the wrong-doers whom Rob Howden, the constable, paraded before him. Since he had no lock-up, he was often puzzled to know how to deal with them, and on one occasion when a persistent tramp was brought before him, he said, 'I think, Rob, ye had just better take the lazy blackguard up to Gorgum and wander him there.' He was certainly making the punishment fit the crime, and perhaps he hoped that the vagrant would lose himself thoroughly and come down in somebody else's lands! There was very little else that could be done about offenders, since part of Galashiels lay within the parish of Melrose and Rob Howden might chase his man through the barony only to see him cross the road into freedom while he could do nothing but stand and watch him escape; and, as Galashiels was beginning to grow, there were more men to start brawls after taking a *dram*, and more boys to climb garden walls in search of green apples and stomach-aches.

You have probably read about the services which feudal tenants had to perform for the lord of the manor in earlier times, and you may have thought that all such arrangements had died out centuries ago. But in fact, some services were often still a condition of holding land in 1800. (On farms, for example, tenants might have to pay *kain* to their landlords, or to perform a *darg*: kain was the provision of a certain number of tame fowls each year, and a darg was a compulsory day's labour by a man or woman. A man might have to do a day's ploughing and a woman a day's spinning for their landlord.) When George Mercer signed a ninety-nine years' lease of Wilderhaugh Mill with the laird, John Scott of Gala, one of the conditions laid down was that if the Mercer family lived in the mill-house they must grind at the mills of Galashiels 'all the Corns Malt and Wheat which they shall make use of' and that they must also 'buy at the said Mills all the Meal they shall have occasion to buy . . . provided it be as good and cheap as in Galashiels Market.' Probably George Mercer was not much worried about having to grind corn and buy meal at the laird's mill, but the condition showed that the laird had a power over the daily lives of his tenants which we would now find annoying. This had its other side, of course, because the laird took a greater interest in the townsfolk and their affairs than most modern landlords are expected to show.

Near to the gates of Gala House stood the parish church, whose minister, with the *Kirk Session,* kept a watchful eye on the people of the village. In times gone by, the Kirk Session had been very severe, and although we can understand this when really serious matters were involved, we find it less easy to do so when we hear of public rebukes to church members for sitting up late in their own houses playing cards, or to a woman for drawing water from the well on a Sunday.

In 1800, however, things were very much easier. Much of the old severity had gone, and the minister, Dr Douglas, was a man who did everything he could for the welfare of the people, both as Christians and as workers. He was particularly interested in helping the weavers to improve their conditions, and they felt that they could rely on his help, as you can see from this letter, written in 1789 by a group of weavers to him:

'Sir—Wee supos that you have heard the repited Complents of oure Cloths being so narow which oblidged us to adapt the lids plan in Erecting Fly Shuttls and indeed many of us is standing indeted to the Tradesman for the expence oing to our want of Stok . . . The read makers tell us nothing but stiell reads will stand which is altogether out of our pour to purchiss and we are persuaded that if the matter was represented to the Honrable boord of Trustes by any kind person they could len ther aid to purchiss such a nesaser thing, for unless we be helpit wee will be redused to our old way . . .'

You will not find this very easy to understand until you have read the chapters about the making of cloth; if you are unable to work out what the weavers were saying, you will find their letter in today's spelling on page 92.

The tactful way in which they appealed for the help of 'any kind person' had its reward, and Dr Douglas took up their cause, with the result that the Board made several grants of £20 between 1789 and 1796 for replacing wooden *reeds* with steel ones.

When the Board granted money for the building of a house for drying cloth, the minister and the Kirk Session were appointed to see that it was properly run. We can imagine the outcry which there would be today if it were suggested that, for example, the local bus service was to be run by the parish minister and his Kirk Session! But in 1800, there was no burgh council in Galashiels to organize public works, and there were very few people who could do so. The laird, the minister and the dominie were the most obvious ones, and it was natural that the Board of Trustees should ask Dr Douglas to watch over the work of the new drying house since he had already spoken up for the weavers.

If the laird and the minister seemed important to adults in Galashiels, the dominie, Mr Robert Fyshe, was a figure of awe to the pupils in the Burgh school—as well he might be with his shaggy eyebrows and his 'firm and determined mouth', not to mention his reddish-brown wig. If we can believe what one pupil of the school wrote, Mr Fyshe did not think very highly of them. ' "Lubbert, dunderhead," were the usual epithets shouted by the master, while the tawse raised clouds of dust from the jackets of pupils as tall as himself.'

However, he seems, with the help of one assistant, in one room, to have taught as many subjects as are on the timetable of any secondary school today; for when the school was inspected in 1819, the 137 pupils were examined in 'English, grammar, spelling, reciting, Latin, Greek, French, British history, antiquities, modern geography, mathematics with their application to mensuration, plain and spherical trigonometry, algebra, mechanics, etc., astronomy and use of the globes, arithmetic, book-keeping and writing'. After this, it is rather surprising to hear that pupils had time to spend in 'gambling at odds or evens for cherry-stones, trafficking in knives, tops, marbles, etc., or in adjusting the preliminaries of a fistic encounter after school hours'.

You may think that, in a place like Galashiels, there can have been very little for school-children to do in their free time except to pick fights, which is all that is meant by 'fistic encounters', but they and their elders had their amusements and excitements, even though we might not think very much of them.

For one thing, they had markets in March, at Midsummer

and at Martinmas. These were mainly for the sale of seed-corn, sheep, wool, cheese and black cattle, according to the season of the year; but they were always great occasions for a place like Galashiels, with a solemn proclamation of the fair from the Tolbooth, the narrow streets filled with people, frightened sheep and cattle being herded into pens for sale, dogs slinking at their

A Fair

master's heels or in at the tail of the flock to round up a straggler with a sharp nip, bargains being struck, shouting and bleating and barking—and the fifteen licensed houses doing a roaring trade.

For shepherds, fairs meant business, but also the chance of a *crack* with their friends from other farms; for shopkeepers, it meant trade; for children, it meant a break in the routine of

Tam O'Shanter and Souter Johnny

school or mill; and for the 'cutters of purses, *Egyptians* and *randy* beggars', who had been warned off when the fair was proclaimed, it meant the chance of quick money for a moment's skilful work.

Then, Shrove Tuesday (known as *Fastern's E'en*) had its celebrations, which were really a survival of the Carnival which, before the Reformation, had brought in the fast-days of Lent. In Galashiels, there was a game of football or handball which was no tidy seven-a-side affair, but was rather more like the Eton Wall-game. On one occasion when Mr Walter Scott helped to arrange a handball game in which Galashiels and Selkirk men took part, there were no less than a hundred men on each side and the goals were a mile apart! Tempers rose so high when the Galashiels men changed sides that the game had to be abandoned and an angry mob stopped Scott's carriage in Selkirk Square because they thought that he had been responsible for the change of sides. However, he was able to buy his safety by handing them two guineas to buy themselves a drink. So these games were not for weaklings.

Sometimes, too, on Fastern's E'en, the banqueting chamber at the Fleece Inn was turned into a cockpit for the evening. A ring of turf was laid on the floor, and feathers flew and blood was shed as the men of Galashiels cheered on their sharp-clawed fighting-cocks against those of Selkirk.

As the days shortened, about Michaelmas, the whole of Galashiels turned out to watch the last big celebration of the year—the annual procession of the Manufacturers' Corporation. This was an occasion for everybody in the woollen trade: for the children, who led the procession: for the weavers in their best clothes, following their banner: and for the officers of the Corporation, wearing their silk sashes and defended by two *halberds* and a drawn sword. You might suppose that they would march to a drum-and-fife band, but, in spite of the sword and halberds, this was a peaceful procession, and the band was composed completely of fiddles! However, on one occasion at least, John of Skye, the Abbotsford piper, added the skirl of the pipes to the scrape of the fiddles, which must have made an unforgettable sound. The day always ended with a great public dinner, at which as many as a hundred adults might sit down, quite apart from the '70 boys and girrels' whom we read of in one year's account.

Very occasionally, something happened which threw the whole village into an uproar. On the night of 31 January 1804, the beacon which had been built on the Eildon hills above Melrose suddenly flared up, the alarm bell on the Galashiels Tolbooth rang out, and from all directions the Volunteers, who were the local militia, hurried to muster for the defence of the county against the French! An eyewitness told afterwards of the scene that night. 'Women were to be seen helping their men with their *accoutrements*, some rinnin' wi' ae thing an' some wi' anither, sabbin' and *greetin'* a' the time, while the bairns were haudin' by their gown tails cryin' for their faithers no' to leave them.'

But at last, the Volunteers, forty-strong including Rob

Howden, the parish constable, were ready to march; and on a baggage-waggon, refusing to dismount, was Susie Hall, the sergeant's wife, who, having followed the drum from the age of sixteen and faced the French during the Irish Rebellion of 1798, was determined to do so again. Whether she was allowed to go or not, we do not know, but the company finally marched off to rendezvous with other militia-bands at Dalkeith, ten miles south of Edinburgh, leaving Galashiels to be defended by boys and old men; and we must remember that with such bad roads as there were at that time it would hardly have been possible to get help, so we may guess that there was little sleep for anybody in the village that night. Meanwhile, the company marched up Gala Water and across the bleak moorland at its head, and then down the Midlothian River Tyne to Middleton Inn, where they began to hear rumours that it was a false alarm. However, they pressed on to Dalkeith, where they arrived in the morning after a march of nearly thirty miles—only to hear that there was no French invasion. What the Volunteers thought and said, we do not know, but after a rest and a meal they were on their way home again. If they felt weary as they turned the last corner into the village, their hearts must have risen, because the streets were lit up in their honour. They may not have had to fight the French, but they were treated as returning heroes all the same.

But this was the kind of excitement which only came rarely: usually, when the Michaelmas procession and dinner were over, there was little to look forward to but the hard days of winter, when the women would clutch their tartan shawls around them for warmth as they picked their way around the muddy streets on *pattens,* while the men in their *Kilmarnock bonnets* wrapped themselves against the cold in their shepherd *mauds*—the very cloth whose popularity was to set the looms of Galashiels clattering in the 1830s to bring in the prosperity of the new 'tweed' trade.

4 *The Year's Work on a Hill-Farm*

The wool which reached the spinners in Galashiels and other Border villages came from the great flocks of sheep, Black-faced or Cheviot or cross-bred, on the hill-farms. At the end of the eighteenth century the Cheviots, with their short, fine wool, were replacing the Black-faced, whose fleeces were longer, coarser and thinner; but both were to be found, for the Black-faced sheep could survive on a poor diet on the highest moorlands, while the Cheviots preferred the lower pastures and even the poorly drained *haughs*.

The parish minister of Galashiels, Dr Douglas, who wrote an Agricultural Survey in 1798, estimated that, on the 150,000 acres of Selkirkshire sheep-walks, there must be about 120,000 sheep. (He based his estimate on the calculation that one sheep would eat the grass from $1\frac{1}{4}$ acres of pasture each year.) At the same time, he reckoned that, in the parishes of Yarrow and Ettrick, there were 1700 men, women and children!

The hill-farms lay on land drained by two rivers, the Ettrick and the Yarrow, flowing more or less north-eastwards, and the whole area was known as Ettrick Forest. The forest had long ago disappeared, and the hills which rose steeply from the rivers were rounded and green. But their slopes were cut into deep *cleuchs* by small, fast-flowing burns, which could quickly turn into raging torrents after a rainstorm. Heather grew on many of the hills, and there were scattered patches of woodland, where silver birches, rowans and larches grew. The highest summits rose to over 2,000 feet, and here there was mile upon mile of tussocky moorland. In the heart of this country lay St Mary's Loch, three miles long and curved like a boomerang between the steep, green hills, and with waters which could be

Turnpike roads =====
Country roads = = = =

PART OF MIDLOTHIAN

PART OF THE COUNTY OF PEEBLES

Tweed River

Gala Water

GALASHIELS

SELKIRK

PART OF THE COUNTY OF ROXBURGH

Yarrow Water

St Mary's Loch

Ettrick Water

PART OF THE COUNTY OF

peacefully blue at one time and steely grey with wind-whipped
crests on them at another.

Most of the hill-farms lay at least 750 feet above sea-level,
and they varied greatly in size; but 1500 acres would be a
moderate one, while the largest were around 6000 acres.

The farm-houses, low, thatched dwellings, mostly stood near
the mouths of the burns, and miserable places they often were.
Their walls, sometimes of stone and lime, and sometimes of

turf, were no more than six feet high; and the largest of them would be about the size of a modern bungalow, while the smallest would measure about twenty feet by fifteen. Going in by the door, which was near one gable, you would have found yourself in the warm gloom of a *byre*, because the end of the house was occupied by a cow tied up to a manger with her tail towards the door. All winter long, the shepherd's family heard her rustling and stamping and lowing, for she was only shut off from the rest of the house by the backs of the close-beds. These were bedsteads, six feet long and four feet wide, with a frame six feet high, rather like a four-poster bed; but instead of curtains they had solid wood panels down one side and at the head and foot, and doors on the other side. By day, they looked, with their doors closed, rather like cupboards; and at night, when the family went to sleep, they could leave the doors open to get a breath of air, or shut themselves in for warmth. Between the beds, there was a narrow passage through

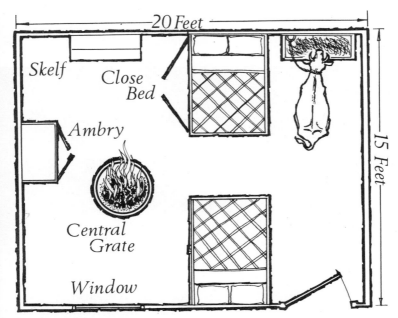

Plan of a labourer's cottage about 1800

which they passed from the byre to the kitchen. In some houses, the fireplace was still in the centre of the room in a round grate, with a lath-and-plaster chimney-hood, in the shape of a funnel, coming down from the ceiling to within five feet of the floor to carry away the smoke. Round this grate the whole family sat—the man of the house in a wooden armchair, and the rest on stools—and over the fire hung the family's one cooking pot, with porridge or mutton broth boiling in it, or the girdle, on which pease-meal or barley bannocks slowly baked dry.

The wife had little else: a wooden bucket for water, a churn, and two barrels, one for salted mutton and one for meal. Her crockery was kept on a shelved frame called a 'skelf', which hung on one wall, and her larder was called an *ambry*; but there were not many left-overs in a diet of porridge and milk, bannocks and cheese, and salt mutton boiled in a broth with kale!

It was from such cottage-kitchens as these that shepherds set off day by day with their dogs to walk the hills and see that all was well with the flocks, and you can see from the picture what

The Penny Wedding

bare places they were, even when the family was making merry.

The pastures stretched away up above the cottages on to the moorland, where only an occasional dry-stone *dyke* marked off one farm from another. Scattered here and there on the moors or in the cleuchs were round, stone-built enclosures about ten yards in diameter and six feet high, with an open gateway. These were 'stells' or refuges, where the sheep could find shelter—and a bite of hay, if the farmer knew his business— in winter storms.

The year's round began in November, when the *tups* were put in with the ewes. The farmer would hope that two-thirds of his ewes would lamb each year, for with losses from the flock at 2 per cent at least, in a good year, and averaging 7 per cent when good and bad years were taken together, he could not keep his numbers up otherwise and make any profit from sales.

From December to March, the flocks roamed the whole of the farm, and the shepherd was lucky if he did not have to go out in bitter snow-storms, at the risk of his own life to dig his flocks out of drifts.

We know something about the winter weather and the losses which it brought to farmers from two shepherds who wrote

Blackfaced or Scot's Ram

about their experiences, James Hogg, 'the Ettrick Shepherd', and the shepherd of Bowerhope farm, Alexander Laidlaw.

James Hogg measured every storm by the memory of the most terrible one of all, which was known as 'The Thirteen Drifty Days'. Though it had happened over one hundred years before, probably in 1674, that storm was still talked of, and the tale was handed down from father to son of how snow had begun to fall one freezing March day and had gone on, all through the night, driving down on the half-starved flocks huddling in the lee of the hills. It fell day after day and night after night, drifting deeper and deeper, for nearly a fortnight, while the shepherds and their dogs struggled out into the blizzard, trying to find the flocks and drive them down to shelter round the farm-steadings. But the sheep, terrified and numbed by the cold, would not move, so, as time went by, the shepherds began to make a little shelter for some of them by building the carcases of those which had died into semi-circular walls against the endlessly-falling snow. Behind the walls, as they rose higher, the survivors, frantic with hunger, tore at each other's fleeces with their teeth. When, finally, the flakes stopped whirling down and the sheep could be dug out, a few lean beasts tottered out from behind the walls of stiffened carcases; and when the losses were counted up, it was reckoned that nine out of every ten sheep throughout the south of Scotland had died.

Nothing was ever quite so terrible as the memory of that storm, but in 1794 snow fell for 20 hours on 24 January, and 'many men' were killed, while Bowerhope lost thirty sheep in one night. In 1799, when the weather was very severe up till late May, Sundhope lost 66 per cent of new-born lambs and 33 per cent of ewes, Bowerhope lost 40 per cent of lambs and $7\frac{1}{2}$ per cent of ewes, and Bridgend, in Megget, lost 50 per cent of lambs and 20 per cent of ewes. Both these years were very bad ones, but Alexander Laidlaw, who had studied records of weather handed down for two hundred years, reckoned that one year in six was likely to be a bad one, so the winter was always an anxious time for shepherds. When you look at these figures of losses in 1799, you have to remember that, on Bowerhope for example, there would not only be far fewer lambs to sell in the later summer for meat, but there would be fewer ewes to breed from in 1800. This would mean fewer lambs born than usual, and so you can see that it would take quite a long time to build up the numbers in the flock again. And, of course, lower numbers meant less fleeces to be clipped and sold. So the loss would be felt for several years.

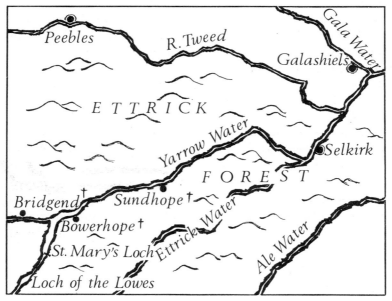

Ettrick and Yarrow
Names marked with a † are those of farms mentioned in this chapter

At the end of March, the *great-ewes* were separated from the rest of the flock, and in April the lambing began. The careful shepherd built an enclosure for his great-ewes and lambs, so that they did not suffer from the bitter winds which might come blasting down the narrow cleuchs. From April till July, the ewes suckled their lambs, which were then weaned and divided into two groups. Some were kept as 'holding stock' (i.e. they were to be added to the flock) and they were branded on the face with the farmer's initial and had a 'lug-mark' cut on their
C

ear, so that, wherever they might wander on the moors, each shepherd could easily tell his own flock. The rest of the lambs were sold and might fetch 5s each.

July was a specially busy time for the hill-farmer. First, there was the sheep-washing, which was done in preparation for the clipping. If there was a pond on the farm, the sheep were driven through it; otherwise, a burn would be dammed with stones to make a pool and the sheep would be sent from one side to the other. This took away the loose dirt on the fleeces, but it was not very thorough and the wool was scoured properly at the mill. However, the washed fleeces fetched a better price in the market than dirty ones.

Then came the shearing. All the sheep, except for the new lambs, were clipped and this was such a big job that several shepherds would help each other; so, at each farm in turn, the sheep were driven into pens by quick, intelligent sheep-dogs; the shearers worked as quickly as they could; piles of fleeces were baled up; newly clipped sheep, startlingly white, were turned out to the pastures; and dust and shouts rose in the air from morning till night. When the work was done, the shepherds who had come to help would whistle up their dogs and tramp off into the dusk, and the way home no doubt seemed

Whitefaced or Cheviot Ram

longer or shorter according to the refreshment which their host had given them before they set out.

Then the farmer might ride or walk miles to one of the great markets which were just beginning, to sell his lambs and wool and even, perhaps, some cheese made from the milk of his ewes. He might go north to Peebles or might cross into Clydesdale for the St James's Fair at Lanark, but he was more likely to go south to Hawick or east to St Boswells or even Kelso. Very often stock and goods were not shown for sale, but were sold 'by character', which meant that they fetched a price according to what was known about the farmer and his farm. It was a good enough way of doing business, for a man could soon lose his name for fair dealing if the goods did not come up to standard when they were delivered.

In August came the hay-harvest, but at this time this was not always thought very important on a hill-farm; and a writer about farming said that losses could be greatly reduced if shepherds would make hay on the low-lying fields for feeding in the stalls after November.

Early autumn saw more markets, this time for *cast-ewes*. These were of no more use for breeding but could be sold for around ten shillings each after a little fattening. Meanwhile, the sheep and lambs sold earlier on started the long journey to their new owners. Nowadays, of course, sheep are transported quickly in trucks from place to place; but for Alexander Laidlaw and his fellow-shepherds, moving sheep could only be done at the flock's own pace, and this, in spite of the sheep-dogs nipping at the heels of the laggards as they turned aside to graze by the road, was very slow indeed. On a dry day of late August or early September, the flock, with its shepherd and his dogs, moved along leisurely in a sunlit haze of dust kicked up by the sheep's trotters on the unmade road.

Finally, at Martinmas, with the first chill of winter, came the 'smearing' or 'salving', when the sheep and lambs had a mixture of tar and butter rubbed into the roots of the fleece. With five gallons of tar and thirty-six pounds of butter, a shepherd could smear fifty young or seventy old sheep at $4\frac{1}{2}$d each. There were those who thought that smearing was not only a messy business but a useless one as well, but many farmers believed that it protected the sheep from the cold and damp of winter by 'waterproofing' the fleece. (You will remember having met with 'tarred wool' near the beginning of this book, where there is a list of places and the kind of woollen goods which were made there.)

When the newly-tarred sheep had been turned out once more on the hills, the farmer could settle down to work out how much he had made by all his hard work. First, he wrote down all the money he had paid out in various ways; then, he made a list of all that he had made from sales; and then, he took away his expenses from his sales to find his profit for the year.

Here are the accounts of a farmer with a flock of 2000 ewes, thirty *gimmers*, 400 *ewe-hogs* and twenty tups. He did not own his farm, but rented it from a landowner. When we rent a house or some land nowadays, the rent has something to do with the size: a larger house or a larger field generally costs more in rent than a smaller one in the same place. The hill-farmer's rent was reckoned by deciding how much it cost to feed a sheep for a year on that farm and multiplying that figure by the number of sheep in the flock. (You can work this out from the accounts.)

When the farmer took a lease of the farm, the flock was already there, and belonged to the landowner; but since he had had to buy it at some time in the past, he recovered that expense by charging the farmer for the use of it at five per cent of the purchase price per year. (Again, you can work out from the accounts how much the landowner had paid for the flock.)

Expenses

	£	s	d
Rent at 3s 6d per sheep	350	0	0
Interest on purchase price of flock at five per cent	58	19	0
Smearing at 4½d per sheep	37	10	0
Wages of three shepherds at £20 each	60	0	0
Upkeep of drains, stells, etc., and mole-catching	15	0	0
	£521	9	0

	£	s	d
120 great-ewes at 14s 6d	87	0	0
200 cast-ewes at 11s	110	0	0
800 lambs at 5s	200	0	0
1800 fleeces at 2s	180	0	0
Cheese, tups, *morts*, etc.	50	0	0
	£627	0	0

Profit: £105 11s 0d

When a farmer with a fair-sized flock made a profit of little more than £100, we may guess that there were many who made still less and for whom a bad winter might mean no profit at all. Little wonder that the hill-farmer's house was a comfortless place and that he and his family lived on the same monotonous diet of broth, salt mutton, cheese and porridge, milk and bannocks year in and year out!

5 The Manufacturers' Corporation

Long before the time of the Mercers, the Lees's and the Sandersons there had been weavers in Galashiels, and in 1666 they banded together to protect themselves against anyone who might wish to steal or harm their trade. There were all sorts of societies like this in England and Scotland, and some of them had very splendid names, such as the 'Company of Blacksmiths, Lorimers, Locksmiths, Cutlers and Bladesmiths' or the 'Society of Armourers and Brasiers'; but the weavers, being plain Scotsmen, simply called themselves the Weavers' Corporation.

You might think that there were so few of them at that time that their trade would hardly be worth protecting; and you might also wonder who could damage it, in any case. Of course it is true that the trade was very small, but it was their livelihood, and if it were stolen from them they would have no other skill to fall back on. So they were trying to protect themselves by preventing people from practising as weavers who were not properly trained—because if anybody could set up as a weaver there would not be enough work to go round and the work might be badly done. In the end, everybody would suffer by the bad work of unskilled men.

We do not know very much about these weavers and their Corporation, but they did leave a list of the equipment which they held in common, and the interesting thing about this list is that some of the items on it are still used today. *Shuttles*, reeds and *caulms* are all part of the weaver's trade still, even though they have changed in appearance and have been improved on since then. But the job which they do has not really altered very much in three hundred years.

Over a hundred years later, on 'the Last Day of December One Thousand Seven Hundred and Seventy seven years', some manufacturers met and decided to form their own corporation. These manufacturers were weavers themselves, of course, and you must not think of them as sitting back in comfortable offices and giving orders, while others got on with the actual work. They were simply weavers who, like their fellows, came from nothing, and who worked as hard as any of the men whom they employed; but they were also men with the extra ability which was needed to organize others, to build machine-sheds, to find a market for their goods and, with nothing behind them but their own skill, to take risks.

These were the men who came together on the last day of December 1777 to form a Manufacturers' Corporation; and, since this was an important moment, 'immediately a *Seal of Cause* was wrote upon stampt paper by Mr Jas. Blaikie School-master & signed by Mr Scott of Gala'. Whether Mr Blaikie was there to put their aims into good English, or whether it was just that he wrote more clearly than anybody else since that was part of his job, we do not know; but once their resolution was written on 'stampt' paper, it was a legal document—and you will notice that the laird signed it, which meant that he showed his approval of having a Manufacturers' Corporation in his barony.

The aims of the Corporation were very much the same as those of the weavers of 1666, and we know a good deal more about the way in which they went about their business, because they kept regular minutes and accounts.

By 1790, there were twenty-three members, and in that year they agreed that each must bind his apprentices by an *indenture* within fourteen days on penalty of a half-crown fine. We do not know why this rule was made, but it looks as if some boys entering the trade were not being taught properly and were being allowed to become journeymen without knowing the work thoroughly. And this, of course, was bad for the trade. It is easy to see why some masters might avoid binding boys as apprentices, because once a boy was indentured, his master was obliged to teach him all about the trade—including its secrets—and to have him boarding in his house, eating as only a hungry boy can eat, and giving him, for some years at least, very unskilled help. He would be breaking threads, making mistakes in his weaving and taking twice as long over the job as a skilled man. And when he came out of his apprenticeship and could practise his trade as a journeyman, he might seek his fortune elsewhere, leaving his master high and dry. So some masters may have been employing boys without binding them as apprentices because it seemed cheaper and easier to do so, and the Corporation was trying to stop this happening.

At the same time, it tried to encourage its members to send their eldest sons into the trade by making the entry fees cheaper for them than for other boys. Their idea may have been that once the eldest son had become an apprentice, the others were more likely to follow; so the charges were like this:

	Apprenticeship fees	*On becoming journeymen*
Eldest sons	nothing	2s 6d
All other boys	2s 6d	5s 0d

Although the Corporation made it easy for the eldest sons of members to enter the trade, it did not hesitate to fine the members themselves if they stayed away from meetings: only a shilling or two, it is true, but that was probably enough to keep most of them up to the mark and it also helped to raise money. But the main idea behind the fines seems to have been to make sure that members took their part in the Corporation. It would have been very easy for such a small, weak organization to wither away if members had felt they could please themselves as to whether they attended meetings or not; so the fines persuaded them to attend, just as the free apprenticeships of their eldest sons helped to keep up their connection with the trade.

The Corporation had its officials, of course, and their names appear in lists, year after year. So, in 1790–91, we find:

Wm Johnston	Deacon
John Lees	Boxmaster
Geo. Mercer	Qr master
John Roberts	do.

Edinburgh: the Lawnmarket

'Deacon' was the name given to the year's chairman, and it went the rounds of the most important manufacturers' families, the Mercers, the Lees's, the Sandersons and others. (It is safe to say, however, that none of them made such a name for himself as the famous Deacon Brodie of Edinburgh, who had, in 1788, finished a remarkable double career as master cabinet-maker and master-burglar on the gallows in the Lawnmarket!)

The Boxmaster was the Treasurer and the Quartermasters probably looked after the social activities of the Corporation, such as the Michaelmas dinner.

Like the weavers of 1666, the Manufacturers' Corporation had a list of 'Articles belonging to the Trade', and these were 'a *Teazing Willie*, a Grinding Stone, a pr. of Smiths Bellows, a Flag or Colour with Sashies &c. for the Annual procession, a Chist for holding do.'

The Willy was one of the machines used in making wool ready for spinning, and in 1780 some of the manufacturers clubbed together and bought one for the use of everybody. They set it up, at first, in John Roberts's garret, but they let it out each year to a different member for a few shillings, and he could charge fellow-members a small sum for having their wool teazed. So everybody was satisfied: the Corporation earned a little money from the rent of the willy, each member had the chance of renting it for a year and making something by teazing wool for others, and the willy was looked after properly, because it had to be given back in good condition at the end of the year.

The grindstone was not let out to anybody but members could have the big shears which they used for clipping the nap on finished cloth sharpened for 'one penny sterling'; while weavers who were not members could have theirs sharpened too—at a shilling a time!

In March, 1791, the Corporation made a big decision, which was to build a Cloth Hall. Although the Minutes do not say so, the idea seems to have been to make Galashiels into a cloth-marketing town as well as a cloth-making one, by providing a hall in which sellers could display their goods and buyers could inspect cloth from several manufacturers before they made their choice. (This was not the usual way of marketing cloth in the Scottish woollen trade. In fact, it was rather like the system in the Yorkshire trade, where most of the cloth was sold in cloth halls.)

Nowadays, months would go by while planning permission was being obtained and plans were being drawn up for a building like this, but in 1791, it was a case of no sooner said than done. An advertisement was put out for tenders for 'the mason and wright work slating and plaistering' and it called on tradesmen to attend with their estimates 'at the house of Thomas Cleghorn Galashielsmiln on Saturday May 7 1791 at four o clock afternoon when they will be taken into consideration and a bargain concluded'. The Corporation was as good as its word, too, for the Minutes for that day give the names of

'John Sanderson & Adam Paterson both in Galashiels for the

Mason work, John Hitton Darnick Wright, Thos. Darling Slater Hawick, Sibbald Plasterer do.' It is rather surprising that they had to go as far afield as Hawick, about fifteen miles away, for a slater and a plasterer and that none of the seventeen joiners in Galashiels could make a low enough estimate to win the job, so that it went to a man in Darnick, on the outskirts of Melrose. However, the men who won the tenders on that Saturday afternoon 175 years ago were no eighteenth-century jerry-builders, and they put up a hall which is still standing.

On 4 June the foundation stone was laid. 'The Corporation with a number of patriotic Gentlemen walked in procession from the deacon's to the Cross & laid the foundation stone with the usual ceremonys, then retired to Mrs Craig's & spent the remaining part of the evening in the most *convivial* manner.' And a remarkably cheap evening it was too, for, as the Corporation's accounts tell us, the sum of 9s was spent on wine!

Of course, the twenty-three members could not have taken on such a big undertaking as this on their own, and they appealed for subscriptions. As the building went on, in the summer and autumn of 1791, the money came in. There is a long list of subscribers in the Minutes, together with the sums which they gave, from £10 10s 0d, given by 'Capt. Scott of Gala 26th Regiment', down to guineas, half-guineas and even smaller sums from people in Selkirk, Melrose, Kelso and other places in the Borders as far away as Peebles. Some subscriptions came from even greater distances—from Newcastle, Leeds and London. Altogether there were nearly fifty subscribers named in the accounts, and you can see that the idea of a Cloth Hall for marketing woollens in Galashiels interested people far outside the village. All the same, these contributions only added up to about £68; and, although Dr Douglas helped the Corporation with a loan, the members also had to pay some of the expense out of their own pockets.

By 11 October, the Hall was finished and the Corporation was able to hold its annual dinner there, with no less than seventy-two present. On this occasion, as the accounts tell us, £2 was spent on spirits, which, although it was more than was spent at Mrs Craig's on 4 June, still seems hardly enough for seventy-two diners to get very merry on!

The Hall had still to be fitted with shelves for the display of cloth and, as with the willy, the aim was to make money by renting out shelves by the year. Members could each rent up to three of them at 40s per shelf per year, and so could outsiders, but at a higher cost.

The first sale of cloth from the Hall was on 30 July 1792, and 'upwards of 3300 yards were exposed to Sale & mostly the whole were sold in less than ten minutes. The average price was about 3s per yd.' It must have seemed to the Corporation that the risk which they had taken in building the Hall was paying off, but unfortunately the Minutes never tell us anything more about how much cloth was sold through it, and it seems that Galashiels never became a centre for marketing woollens in the way that the Manufacturers hoped.

However, they did make some income out of the Hall, because they rented it out for meetings of various kinds, and even, on one occasion, for a dance. When this income is added to the shelf-rents, to the fees for apprentices entering the trade, to the fines on members who missed meetings, to the rent of the willy and the grindstone charges, the Boxmaster might have the grand total of £10 or £12 to meet the year's expenses.

It was not very difficult for the Corporation to find ways of spending an income of this size, but some of the things which it was spent on may surprise you. For instance, in 1804 and 1805, quite a lot went to pay for a new flag and new sashes. (You will remember that the members wore their sashes and carried their colour at least once a year, in the Michaelmas procession.) In fact, in 1805, nearly the whole of the year's income of £7 6s 4d went on that.

But in other years there were payments which you can perhaps sympathise with more easily. In 1800, 4s was paid 'to a dyer in distress'; in 1806, 3s was given to 'a poor Brother'; in 1809, 3s went to 'a distressed brother'; and in 1810 and 1815 sums like these were paid to other brothers in distress. In other words, the Corporation looked after people in the trade who had fallen on hard times and, in fact, they were prepared to help others as well, for in November 1803 the Boxmaster paid

3s 'to a travler in distress'. These were very small sums, of course, though they bought a great deal more then than they would do now, but they were only meant to be a stop-gap. They were not meant to give regular benefit like National Insurance today but were just intended to keep a man or a family from complete destitution. Parish Relief in Scotland was not meant to help the able-bodied poor and there were no workhouses for them to go into; so, in bad times, they could suffer terrible hardships, and in this case even a payment of 3s must have been a godsend. With it, a man could keep a roof over his family's heads, and if they had meal for porridge, and some bones, barley and potatoes for broth they would survive—or the strongest of them would, at least.

Scrapin' Taties

Even so, there was a feeling that you should not help the poor too much or they would not help themselves. As one minister wrote at the time: 'A spirit of extravagance has infected the lower ranks in the parish of Selkirk and they expend most of their wages on finery and pleasures and depend on receiving support from the parish in poverty and old age.' Since parish relief was so wretchedly mean, the money doled out now and again by the Corporation must have been welcome to those in distress.

Another way in which the Boxmaster spent some of the year's income was in the upkeep of the tools of the trade. The willy never seems to have given any trouble, but the grindstone cost the Corporation quite a lot of money in 1793-95 and again in 1808. A grindstone was not just any lump of stone, of course. Some kinds of rock would be quite useless because they would split or flake, which, apart from being very dangerous to the user, would damage the blade. Sandstone was often used, and in fact we know that grindstones were made at Craigleith quarry near Edinburgh and that work was going on there as early as the seventeenth century. Another place where sandstone was used for making grindstones was around Mauchline in Ayrshire. What we do not know is whether the one which was brought to Galashiels in 1808 came from either of these quarries, but it is likely to have been brought from some distance, because the transport of it, in a slow, rumbling, creaking cart over the half-made, pot-holed roads of the time, cost the Corporation nearly £4. When it arrived, there was even more to pay for a new frame for it to stand in—no less than £5 10s 0d. But if this seems a lot to you, you must remember that the stone was very heavy and that it was going to revolve at a high speed, so the frame had to be really solid or it would have fallen to pieces very quickly. Altogether, with 4s 6d for leather (probably for a new driving belt), nearly £10 was spent on fitting up the new grindstone, and that does not include the stone itself, for which no figure was given. This was practically a whole year's income, and it is easy to see why none of the manufacturers had a grindstone of their own: it was too expensive to replace it when it got worn.

Another time, the Corporation might buy new reeds to replace the ones which quickly wore out under the friction of the flying shuttle invented by John Kay; but in one way and another the year's income was easily spent, and there was

Boxmaster.

For the Corporation, the Michaelmas meeting was the great event of the year. It was then that the new Deacon took up his duties, the accounts were balanced and the members dined together in the Cloth Hall or in one of the inns. As time went by, and the Corporation's membership grew, the dinners became larger and larger affairs, with important guests of honour—very different from the evening at Mrs Craig's after the laying of the foundation stone.

In 1821 there were two distinguished guests, when the dinner was held in the Fleece Inn (in the very banqueting room where the cock-fights took place). These were Sir Walter Scott and James Hogg, the Ettrick Shepherd. Before the evening was over, there was a great deal of merriment and singing of Scottish songs. Somebody who was present and was obviously keeping a close eye on the great men said, 'If ye had juist seen hoo Sir Walter rappit the table in time to the tune!' (If everybody was doing so, the rafters of the Fleece Inn must have been shaking with the din!) But that was not all: when called on for a song, he rose and sang the only one which he knew, and which was called 'Tarry Woo'. It seems that Sir Walter could not sing in tune, but his audience must have recognized the words, whatever the song sounded like. The second verse was a reminder to everybody present of the work which went on day in, day out before there could be any celebration:

> 'Tarry Woo, Tarry Woo
> Tarry Woo is ill to spin;
> *Card* it weel, card it weel
> Card it weel ere ye begin;
> When 'tis carded, row'd and spun
> Then the work is *halflins* done;
> But when woven, drest, and clean,
> It may be *cleading* for a queen.'

The dinner that year was such a success that Sir Walter was asked again in 1822, and the invitation came in the form of a poem:

> ' "This year we rather 'gin to falter
> If an epistle we should send you.
> Say some, "Ye only plague Sir Walter,
> He canna *ilka* year attend ye."
>
> "He's dined but lately wi' the king,
> And round him there is sic a splendour
> He *winna* stoop to such a thing
> For a' the reasons you can render." ' '

After that rather nervous opening, the poet goes on to tell Sir Walter that the menu will be according to his tastes:

> ' "Your favourite dish is not forgot:
> *Imprimis*, for your bill of fare,
> We'll put a sheep's head in the pot—
> Ye'se get the *cantle* for your share:
>
> 'And we've the best o' "*Mountain Dew*",
> Was gathered where ye maunna list
> In spite o' a' the *gauger's* crew
> By Scotland's "children o' the mist." ' '

Whether Sir Walter attended the dinner and ate his cantle of sheep's head, we do not know; but perhaps he felt that as Sheriff of Selkirkshire he could hardly be seen drinking whisky from an illicit still and so cheating the exciseman, even at the Corporation's Michaelmas dinner!

We should not feel very pleased to be invited to a dinner where the main dish was boiled sheep's head. But of course Galashiels in 1822 was still little more than a village, where the elegance which would be found in the handsome houses of Edinburgh's New Town would be out of place. To the Manufacturers' Corporation of Galashiels, a dinner of sheep's head chased down by whisky was an enjoyable way of celebrating the end of one year's work for the improving of the trade and the beginning of a new one.

6 In the Mill: Raw Wool to Carded Sliver

Between the day when a manufacturer like George Mercer struck a bargain with a farmer at one of the wool-sales and the moment when a piece of cloth, three-quarters of a yard wide and twenty or twenty-one yards long, came from the loom, a lot of hard work was done by many people.

The fleeces came down the valley to Galashiels baled into tight packs, sometimes by pack-horse and sometimes in carts; but either way, they would be dumped in a shed at the mill for sorting. When we talk of a mill, however, we have to be sure what the word meant to the people of Galashiels.

Pack-ass

The earliest mills, which were in existence in 1580, were called *waulk-mills,* and they were places where cloth was 'fulled' or 'felted', to thicken it. The fulling was all that was done at the mill and it was such a primitive building that its side-walls were not even made up. It was just a long trough with a roof over it for shelter—but in winter the floor all round it might be slippery with mud or ice, so it must have been a wretched place to work in.

When George Mercer signed a *tack* with the young laird, John Scott of Gala, in 1800, Wilderhaugh consisted of a covered waulk-mill together with a new building put up in the 1780s. This was built of stone from the Gala estate and was sixty-five feet long, with a slated roof—a very uncommon sight at that time—and it combined a mill-house and a machinery house. At the time when it had been built, most of the work was still being done by hand, or by hand-driven machines. The willy was a hand-driven one; hand-carding was done by a method which had not altered very much for centuries; and spinning was done on wheels. Water-power was only used to drive the mallets which had taken the place of human feet in pounding the finished cloth to felt it. (There were other mills, of course, in Galashiels, which used water-power to grind corn and meal.)

It is easy to talk of using water-power, but how did George Mercer get water to work for him in Wilderhaugh? If you look back at the map of Galashiels, you can see that there are two waterways through the village—Gala Water itself, and the mill-lade. North of the town (and off the map), there had been built what was known as a 'cauld', which was rather like a weir. A dam was built across the river so as to raise the water-level just enough to run it off into a lade. Since Gala Water, like many Scottish streams, flowed rather quickly, an apron was built, sloping out from the dam, so as to carry the water away gently, otherwise there was a danger that it would fall straight down and undermine the dam. Meanwhile the lade filled up with water and a *sluice-gate* which was placed across the entry from the river allowed the flow to be regulated.

The mill-lade carried the water down through the village,

passing Wilderhaugh and Mid Mill and others as they were built, and each mill used it to drive a wheel. Sometimes, where a mill stood rather low down on the bank, the water might be channelled in so as to fall on the wheel from on top, as in this picture; and this was called an overshot wheel.

Water-wheel, overshot

At other places, a mill might stand rather high above the lade, and in that case the wheel was built so that the water would strike it directly from the side—at about 9 o'clock, so to speak. This was an undershot wheel.

The wheel had shallow buckets all round its circumference, and, whether it was overshot or undershot, the water hit and filled each of them in turn, and this made the wheel revolve. As it did so, water emptied itself out of each bucket, which was then carried round to the top again.

But the wheel was not kept turning all the time. The water could not always be channelled down the lade, since this

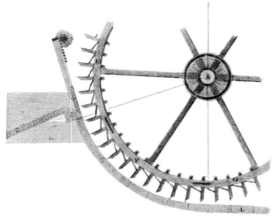

Water-wheel, undershot

would have taken too much out of the main stream, so the
sluice-gate was only opened at intervals. The water would then
flow in and would be brought to each mill-wheel through its
own small damhead. In order to share the flow of water fairly
between the different mills, there had to be agreements about
the amount which each could use. In some places, the right
to use water was shared out equally, but in others there might
be only one person who was allowed to open the main sluice,
and you can see how this could lead to bad blood if it was thought
that he was doing so for his own advantage. Water-rights were
so important that they counted as part of the assets of a mill
when it changed hands, and a value in money was put on them
—and this might go into several hundreds of pounds.

When the wheel was turning, its movement was usually
passed on to the mill-machinery in one of two ways. In the
one case, a slowly-turning shaft ran from the axle of the water-
wheel, and its cogged head meshed with much smaller cogs
on a second shaft which ran into the machinery-house of the
mill. This was the 'line-shaft', and since its cogs were much
smaller than those of the axle-shaft, they revolved much faster
and gave the *revolutions* which were needed to run machines at
high speeds. The machines were linked to the line-shaft by
48 pulleys.

Otherwise, the water-wheel would have teeth around its edge, and the line-shaft would mesh into these. For one revolution of the circumference of the water-wheel, the line-shaft would revolve a good many times; so again, the thirty or forty revolutions per minute of the water-wheel would be multiplied a great deal for the line-shaft, and any machine run from it by pulleys would be driven at a high speed.

In the machinery-house of an early factory, probably the only machines in the 1780s were one or two scribbling engines, driven by hand. In another ten years, it would begin to fill up with a willy, a *scribbler* and a carding engine, all driven by pulleys from the line-shaft. By the end of Napoleon's wars, there would be a water-driven machine for raising the nap on the cloth, another for shearing the nap, and a *mule* for spinning.

But now we shall follow the wool which was dumped in packs for sorting, through the processes of manufacture until it went out to the Cloth Hall to be sold, perhaps from George Mercer's shelves.

What a sight there was, when the men slit up the packs and opened out the fleeces! Some of the wool was sticky with tar and grease from the smearing, and some was stained with various colours from plants. It was full of fragments of heather, *whin* and bracken; it was tangled with *burs;* and it was matted with earth and dung. On the outside, the fleece was a stringy mass of grey, where it was not stained, while inside it was shorter, more compact and whiter.

Quickly, the sorters got to work. Their job was not just a matter of picking out the best fleeces. There were differences between the wool of lambs and that of hogs, so they had to be separated from each other. Then each fleece had to be laid out and divided up according to the quality of different parts. The best wool came from the neck and shoulders; on the back it was less good, and what came from the hindquarters, the tail and the back legs was the least good of all. One fleece after another was sorted at high speed, and the bins, each holding wool of one quality, filled up quickly. In one, the wool might be long and rather hard to the feel; in another, there might be wool which was much springier and softer. For making rough blankets a much harder and coarser wool might be used than for weaving cloth for a woman's gown.

Now came the scouring of the wool in a trough filled with a strong soapy solution. This was heavy, dirty work, and in winter the handling of masses of soaking wool must have been a bitterly cold job. The sticky, greasy deposits would only come away with difficulty from the wool, which had to be rinsed again and again until the water was clear—and all this had to be done without any modern washing equipment. The wet wool, heavy as it was, had to be lifted out of the trough for drying, and this could take a long time in damp weather because the wool must dry gently if it was not to become hard and brittle. Anyone who has ever dried a jumper too hurriedly near to the fire knows how easily wool can be ruined.

Although it was now less unpleasant to handle, the wool was not nearly ready for spinning, and the next thing that happened to it was the blending. To a new apprentice, it may have seemed that they were simply undoing the work of the sorters by mixing different lots of wool together, but it was not quite like that. Even where the sorters had several bins of the best quality of neck wool, for example, one might be harder to the touch, or shorter in the *staple,* or with more shine in it. If all this wool was spun into yarn, one bin after another, the quality of the yarn would vary; part of it might be harder or thicker than the rest, and part might have a brighter lustre. The result would be uneven yarn, and, of course, an uneven appearance in the cloth. So, in a corner of the building, a great pile would be made, so many pounds from one bin and so many from another, all carefully weighed out and laid down in layers, so that wherever a slice was taken from top to bottom every quality would be there.

Now they had a pile of white, springy wool which lay all tangled from the scouring; and, since the soap had taken away its natural oil, it had become too silky and smooth to cling together. So, before anything else could be done with it, it had to be teazed, that is disentangled in the willy, and then oiled.

By 1800 George Mercer certainly had his own water-driven willy, which the Board of Trustees had helped him to buy, and so had one or two other manufacturers. But, for the rest, there was the Corporation willy set up in a cottage-garret and driven, probably, by the aching muscles of an apprentice. A Wilder-haugh apprentice had only to carry the wool for teazing over to where the willy stood, a tall cabinet with a hinged flap at the front. Inside, he could see a big cylinder, three feet long with a diameter of $2\frac{1}{2}$ feet. All round its circumference there were spikes. Beneath the cylinder there was a grating, and above it there were either three or five small rollers, fitted with teeth which engaged the spikes on the main cylinder. You can probably see how it worked. When some wool was laid, probably a pound at a time, on the flap which the apprentice had pulled down, it was drawn in and carried round on the spikes of the main cylinder and was thoroughly torn apart as the small teeth meshed with the spikes. So the tangles were teazed out, and this released some of the dust or grit still left in the wool, to fall down the grating. With a water-driven willy, all this happened very quickly. The pound of wool, torn apart as the big cylinder revolved 300 times per minute, was willeyed in three seconds and thrown out on the flap in a light, fluffy mass so that another lot could be put in.

When enough wool had been teazed, the whole fuzzy mass was sprinkled with oil. For high-quality wools, olive-oil might be used, but with the lower qualities something like rape-seed oil was used, while for the poor, stringy wool which could be made into stockings or blankets, the manufacturer might use fish-oil, whose low price compensated for its horrible smell.

Now, although the wool was still light and fluffy, at least it clung together, and it was ready for one of the most important stages in the work—carding. Until this had been done, it would be impossible for a spinner to draw it into a thread, because it would simply come away from the mass in short little bunches.

Carding got its name from the fact that for centuries it had been done by rubbing teazed wool between two 'cards', flat pieces of wood whose faces were covered with what was called 'card-clothing'. This was leather which had a great many very fine teeth stuck into it at an angle so that, when one card was drawn down the other, the wool was pulled out from a mass into thin strands. Sometimes one of the cards was hung from a nail and the other could then be drawn down it with more force. When the spinner took hold of the strand to make it into a thread, she had a length of wool to spin, not a bunch.

But at Wilderhaugh, there was no longer any need for hand-cards, because there were machines to do both parts of the work of carding. By 1800 George Mercer had had a scribbler and a

Carding engine

carding engine brought from England, and they took their power from the mill-wheel. The first part of the work was done by the 'scribbler', which had nothing at all to do with writing but really meant something more like 'scratching' or 'scraping'. It did not look very different from the carding engine which you see here, except that it was made so as to turn the wool out in a different way at the end.

This was a job for a skilled man. Not only did the quality of the yarn depend on how well the wool had been carded, but, for an apprentice, the machines with their rapidly revolving rollers could be dangerous. In England children were sometimes used to clear the wool from the machine at the end, and some of them who did so were not quite skilful enough to avoid losing fingers in the unfenced rollers. Whether any of the younger boys in the Galashiels mills were used for this work, however, we do not know.

Since the scribbler and the carding engine were not very unlike each other, except that the large and small rollers might be arranged differently, there is no need to describe both machines in great detail. Some of the teazed and oiled wool was put on the flat sheet and drawn in until it met the large cylinder which carried it round on its card-clothing. (The whole cylinder was covered with hundreds of little teeth set very carefully so as to hold the wool but not to get clogged up with it.) It passed between the big roller and the small ones, which were also covered with card-clothing, and again, the angle of the teeth varied, because the wool had to be pulled out and drawn into a thinner and thinner sheet with all the fibres lying more or less in one direction. The small rollers revolved at a different speed from the large one and this dragged the wool apart. As the teeth of one small roller meshed with those of the last one, they cleared the wool from it and passed it on over the big cylinder, until it came to the last cylinder, which, on a scribbler, was called the *doffer*. By this time, the wool was travelling in a fine sheet, and as it came round it was combed off the doffer and was then fed into the carding engine. You may wonder why it was necessary to do this, but, for the spinners, the wool had to be as finely carded as possible or the yarn would be uneven and lumpy.

So the sheets of wool passed through the rollers of the carding engine, but when they came to the doffer there were spaces in the card-clothing running the length of the roller. As it revolved, the wool gathered in these spaces, in webs about four inches wide, because there was nothing to grip it and carry it along. They were not turned out of the machine like that, but passed under a final cylinder (the one which is labelled D in the picture) which, as you can see, had shallow channels hollowed out of its surface. When the webs passed underneath it, they were gathered into these flutings; and, as they travelled round, they were formed into ropes about half-an-inch in diameter and twenty-five inches long, before being turned on to the sheet at the end of the machine. These were called slivers, and they were very fragile, of course, because they were not twisted at all and could be pulled apart very easily; but these thick, limp ropes, which were now being wound on to big reels, were soon going to become thin, elastic spun yarn.

To any boy who had just started work, the mill must have seemed a confusion of sights and sounds. He knew about it in a way, before, because he had heard all about it from his father's conversations with work-mates ever since he was a little child, but now that it was happening all round him, it must have been difficult to understand what was going on. There were the bales of dirty fleeces to start with: the scouring and drying; the blending and willying and oiling; the scribbling and carding. It was a mixture of heavy manual labour and of skilled work on the noisy machines, and at first he simply went where he was told to go without really knowing what was going on.

But, for a man born in 1750 or so, who had spent all his working life in the trade, the picture was very different. For most of that time, the only power had been man-power, except in the fulling-mill. Certainly, teazing had become a little easier to do when the willy had been bought and set up in John Roberts's garret—but, even so, it was turned by hand, which must have been hard work. Carding, too, had been a hand-craft up until about 1790, and it needed skill and judgment; besides that, it took a long time to produce enough yarn to keep the spinners busy. But during the 1790s one mill and then others installed machines—scribblers and carding engines—which meant that machine-minding skills had to be learned. For a man in his forties, there was a great difference between handling a pair of cards and tending a machine which might revolve several hundred times a minute. There must have been some who found it difficult to learn these new skills, just as some men who are made *redundant* in their forties today find it very difficult to retrain muscles which for years have been loading coal, for example, to do quite another job. Some may have wished that they could be back in the old waulk-mills with their simple equipment and more restful atmosphere, but the changes had come, and there could be no going back to the old ways.

7 In the Home: Spinning and Weaving

While water-driven machines had made great changes in the early stages of the work, especially in Wilderhaugh, where George Mercer had been quick to try out new inventions, there was one important change which was just beginning in 1790. In that year, he would have sent most of the carded wool out of the mill to be spun on wheels in the cottages in the narrow streets between the mill-lade and Gala Water. The job of a spinner was to draw out the carded sliver to at least twice its own length, twisting it at the same time. The fibres clung together as they were drawn out and twisted, and the slack carding became springy yarn. One way of doing this had been to use a distaff and spindle, but by 1800 very little wool was spun in this way. The most common method was to use a spinning wheel, which drew out the sliver while the spinner's fingers twisted it. But a new way of spinning, where the drawing and twisting were both done by one machine, was to take the place of spinning-wheels, and this was by using the *jenny*. Not only did the jenny draw out and twist the sliver, but it spun a number of threads at the same time. There were still only two spinning-jennies in Galashiels, and, as you may remember from the list of occupations in the village, there were over 200 women who were full-time spinners. Between them, they spun 2916 stones, each of twenty-four English lbs., of wool into yarn, and this was all that was used by the Galashiels looms. By 1798 there were eighteen jennies at work, all of them hand-operated and most of them erected in the lofts of houses; but they were spinning on thirty-six spindles at a time, and, even with stoppages to mend breaks in the yarn, they were steadily making the women's work of spinning on the wheel a thing of the past. Spinning was still a domestic craft: a jenny produced far more yarn than hand-spinning, without having to be set up in a factory. But it did need the complete attention of the spinner to draw out so many threads successfully at the same time, and so it could not be done so easily by women as hand-spinning. A woman could work her spinning-wheel, talk to a neighbour, mind her baby and see that the soup did not boil over, all at one time: she could not do all of these and work a jenny. Hand-spinning and jenny-spinning went on together for quite a long time, and in 1814 the first mules were brought to Galashiels. Mules were very like jennies in some ways, but they also had some features borrowed from another invention called the 'water-frame'. The result was that mules were usually run by water-power and so spinning began to move out of the cottages and into the mills. But between 1790 and 1814 at least, spinning was still done outside the mill on wheels or jennies. In 1833, when the tweed age was just beginning, the 21,000 stones of wool which were used were spun by about thirty-six men and boys, all working on jennies and mules. Hand-spinning, in Galashiels, was dead.

But, since jennies were coming into use in the 1790s, we can take a look into one of those garrets where spinning was done. In fact, the man who was at work there might have been busy on either of the two machines which were used in spinning, for, like carding, it was really done in two stages. The first of these was called 'slubbing' and it produced a coarsely-spun yarn without very much elasticity; the second stage completed the change from the carded sliver, thick and untwisted, to the thin, twisted, springy spun yarn. In both stages, the idea was to draw out the wool, keeping it tight, and twisting it at the same time. The twisting under tension made the fibres cling together so that, when the strain was slackened, the yarn stayed twisted and would spring back if it was stretched again.

In this picture of the slubbing-billy, you can see the slivers travelling up the sheet at the left, and at the right you can see a row of upright spindles. What you cannot see so easily is that each of the slivers passes between two wooden bars before being stretched along the length of the machine and round a spindle.

Slubbing Billy

The man who was working the billy pushed the carriage along on its wheels as far to the left as he could. Then he pulled it back towards himself, and this, of course, pulled out the same length from each of the slivers. Now he brought the two wooden bars together so that they clamped the slivers tight and prevented any more from being drawn out. By pulling the carriage right back to him, he automatically stretched the eight inches or so of sliver which he wanted to twist, and as the length was stretched it became thinner. Meanwhile, he turned the big wheel with his right hand, and the driving belt which ran from it to the spindles made them all twirl round and round, and this twisted the thread slightly. After the carriage was right home, the *slubber* held it still while he kept the spindles turning and so the thread was wound on to them. Then the process began again. As you can see, there were several things to do, and they had to be done skilfully, or else the threads would snap. This was one reason why the job was not very suitable for a woman who had other things to see to at the same time. (Even so, the explanation given here makes it sound a good deal simpler than it really was.)

57

In 1791 George Mercer bought a slubbing-billy with twenty-six spindles, but whether he set it up at Wilderhaugh or whether it was set up in a cottage-loft we do not know. It was only the first of a good many, however, because by 1833 there were sixteen men and eighty children on slubbing, quite apart from the thirty-six men and boys who were spinning.

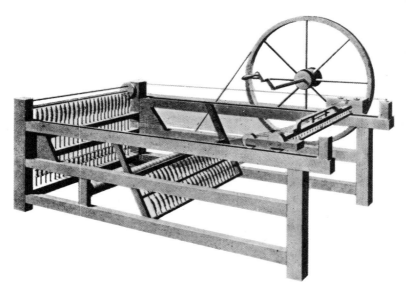

Spinning Jenny

As you can see, the jenny looked very much like the billy, but in fact it was the jenny which was the earlier invention. The jenny was patented in 1770 by James Hargreaves, and the billy came into use a few years later. Both jenny and billy were improved as time went by, and the pictures here are of models which were easier to work than the very first ones. The number of spindles which could be used at one time increased too. Hargreaves's 1770 jenny had about sixteen, but the jenny which George Mercer brought to Galashiels in 1791 had thirty-six, and this was small compared with the giants of over 100 spindles which were the final stage of the jenny's development.

If the man whom we were watching at work in the garret had been a spinner instead of a slubber, you would have seen that his machine was arranged differently—just as the billy and the jenny are in the two pictures. When the slubber finished his work, he had a lot of bobbins full of yarn which was a good deal thicker than the finished thread would be, and only slightly twisted. The spinner, when he received these, mounted them in the slanting frame underneath the jenny, and drew up the slubbings through the two rails on the right, which form the clamp, and then back along the top of the machine to the upright spindles. When he moved the carriage away from him, he pulled up more of the slubbings from their bobbins, and when he clamped it tight and brought it back towards him, he was drawing out his yarn thinner and thinner. So, if he had just finished winding some finished yarn on to the spindles when we found him at work, the carriage of his jenny would have been right over to the left of the picture, and new slubbing would have been pulled out from the bobbins. Now he unclamped the rails and drew the carriage back towards him for several inches, clamped the rails tight again to hold that length of yarn between the spindles and the clamp tight, and drew the carriage back the rest of the way to him with his left hand, while his right set the wheel going to turn the spindles. So he had got his *draft* and his twist: the length of rather thick, slack slubbing was drawn out twice as long at least, and was twisted into springy yarn. The jenny twisted the yarn in the opposite direction from the billy, and you may wonder why this did not simply unravel the slubbing; but the twisting done on the billy had made the wool-fibres cling too closely for them to slip apart, and the further twisting in the opposite direction simply strengthened the yarn. Once the spinner felt that the twisting had gone far enough, he ran the carriage in towards the turning spindles, so that the wool could be wound on to them.

At first, the yarn which was spun on jennies was weak and rather slack, as well as often being lumpy, and it could only be used for the *weft;* but gradually the quality of the yarn improved as the design of the machine was made better. As the number of spindles increased, it began to be necessary to have a 'piecer' working with the spinner to join the threads when they broke, otherwise the jenny would have been continually out of action while the spinner mended them himself. We can easily imagine that, in the early years, a great deal of very coarse weft yarn must have been made in Galashiels, and that a lot of time was lost in joining broken threads before the spinners grew experienced enough to judge the correct tension. But without the jenny, and then the water-driven mule, there could have been no expansion in the woollen trade to feed all the new mouths.

Before handing over the spun yarn, the spinners wound it, from the small bobbins on the jenny, on to larger ones which would hold a good deal more wool. If this had not been done, the weavers would continually have had to stop work to tie in new threads, which would greatly have slowed them down.

Now at last it was the turn of the warper and the weaver. But before we see what they did, we must be sure that we know what weaving is.

The simplest kind of weaving is done when a hole is darned in a sock. First, a needle is passed from end to end of the hole and fills it up with threads running lengthwise. Then the needle is passed from side to side of the hole, over one thread and under the next; and so the space is filled up with a web of woven wool. When a weaver makes a piece of cloth his *warp* threads are the ones running from end to end of the loom. He passes a shuttle, holding a bobbin of yarn, from side to side, over and under the warp threads to make what is called the weft.

The first thing that had to be done was to prepare the warp so that the threads could gradually be wound off a roller called the yarn-beam, which was at the far end of the loom from the weaver, and rolled on to the cloth-beam right in front of him as the cloth was completed. The warper had to wind the warp-threads on to the yarn-beam, and this sounds simple enough until you remember that the piece of cloth was to be about twenty-one yards long by about three-quarters of a yard wide. The width might contain between 600 warp-threads in a very coarse cloth and as many as 1300 in a fine one. So the warper, with the help of at least one boy, had to control perhaps 900 threads and get them all wound at the same tension and in perfect order round the yarn-beam. In unskilled hands, this mass of threads could turn into a cat's-cradle which would never be disentangled.

The way in which he did this was called 'stake-warping'. The warper wound as much yarn as he needed, from bobbins mounted in one frame, round two rows of pegs stuck into a second frame, to give him 900 threads of the right length. As the yarn was wound from side to side down the two rows of pegs and then up again, the threads crossed, and this meant that each one was kept in place by the ones on either side of it. It was important that the threads should stay in their right order when the warp was wound on to the yarn-beam of the loom, because if they got out of place it would be impossible for the weaver to produce cloth without faults in it.

When he had finished winding, the warper laced cords through the warp where the odd threads crossed over the even ones to keep them apart, and then he was able to lift it off the stakes without it all falling into a tangle. Just to help the threads to stand up to the wear and tear of the loom, he dipped the bundle of warp in size, and this stiffened the threads as it dried.

Now the warp, which had been bundled up when it was dry, had to be wound on to the yarn-beam, from which it would gradually unroll in the loom as the weft was woven into it. (This job really needed two people, and probably, at the end of the eighteenth century, it was done by a weaver and an apprentice, though now most of the jobs in the woollen trade are done by workers who specialize in one particular skill.) The ends of the warp threads were passed (still in their proper order) through a framework which had evenly-spaced teeth in it, rather like a comb; and then they were wound, bit by bit, round the yarn-beam, all stretched to the same tightness, so that, at the end of the 'beaming', the warp was regularly spaced along it. Now you can see why the odd threads had been kept separate from the even ones: if they had not been, the warper would not have been able to pass them in the correct order through the framework, and it would have been very easy for

61

threads to get crossed in the loom. Anyone who has darned a hole in a stocking knows how awkward it is if one of the lengthwise threads crosses another one: sooner or later, the point will come when both of them have to be passed over or under, and this makes a fault in the pattern of the darn.

If the yarn-beam had just been put into the loom as it was, and the ends stretched straight to the cloth-beam, the weaver would have had to push the shuttle in and out of the warp threads, just as one pushes a needle over one thread and under the next in darning, and the job would have been impossible. So the yarn-beam was hung at a height convenient for two workers sitting one on either side of it. At about the same height there hung the frames called heald-shafts, and these consisted simply of two rods between which were stretched the caulms—strings with eyelets in them. One of the two workers pushed the ends of the warp-threads, one by one, up to the eyelets in the caulms, and the other one pulled them through; so, if there were 900 warp-threads, they had to be passed through 900 eyelets; and the job was not even as easy as that, because, even in the very simplest piece of weaving, all the odd-numbered ends had to be passed through the caulms on one shaft, and all the even ones through those on another. But when this had been done, half of the warp-threads could be pulled down at

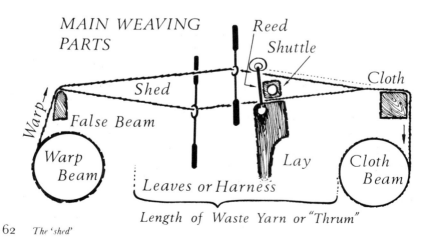

MAIN WEAVING
PARTS

Reed

Shuttle

Cloth

Shed

False Beam

Warp

Warp
Beam

Lay

Cloth
Beam

Leaves or Harness

Length of Waste Yarn or "Thrum"

one time, while the other half stayed still, and this made a space for the shuttle to go through.

Once all the warp-threads had been drawn through the caulms, they were passed, in groups of two or three, between the teeth of a reed. (You will remember how the weavers wrote to Dr Douglas asking him to help them to buy metal reeds instead of the old wooden ones, which were being damaged by the flying-shuttle.) The reeds were shaped much like combs, except that the teeth were fitted into a frame at the bottom as well as the top. When the ends had been passed through the reed, they were tied in bunches, so that it would not drop off them; and then, at last, the whole apparatus—yarn-beam, heald-shafts and reed, with the warp running through them— was ready to be lifted into the loom.

Hand-loom

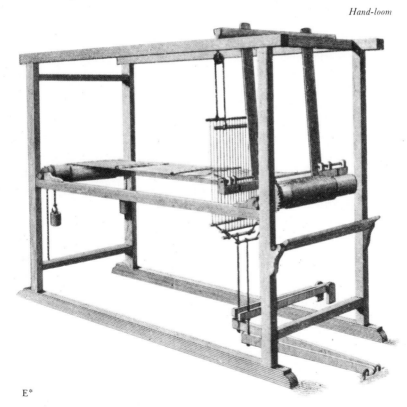

If you look at the picture, you can see the yarn-beam at one end and the cloth-beam at the other. The heald-shafts are hanging straight up and down, one behind the other, with the warp threads passing through the caulms. Underneath the loom, there are treadles and these are connected with the shafts, so that the weaver can pull down the correct shaft by stepping on the right treadle, rather like an organist.

What is not so easy to see is that the reed, through which the warps were passed after being drawn through the caulms, was also fitted into a frame. This hung freely from the frame of the loom and could be swung backwards and forwards against the newly-woven weft so as to beat it firmly up against what had been woven earlier.

When the weaver sat down to his loom, there were several things which he had to do, and, although none of them was very difficult in itself, it was still a very skilled job to combine them all in a smooth sequence so as to produce yard after yard of well-made cloth. (In the same way, you can get two knitters, both of whom know how to do plain and purl stitches, but one of whom knits a beautifully smooth piece of work, while the other's is lumpy and uneven.) First, then, the weaver pressed down one of the treadles, and so pulled down all the threads which passed through the caulms on the shaft connected with it: this was called opening a 'shed' in the warp. If he was making a cloth with a complicated weave, he might have half-a-dozen shafts, and his foot would have to feel its way to the right treadle. When the shed was open, he had to pass the shuttle through it from side to side. Then he brought forward the reed, swinging in its frame from the top of the loom, to 'beat up' the new row of the weft; and, when that was done, he closed the shed. Lastly, he had to work the mechanisms which wound the newly-made cloth on to the cloth-beam and unwound the warp at the correct tension from the yarn-beam.

Before John Kay made his invention, the weaver used to throw the shuttle through the shed, first with his right hand and then back with his left. It did not travel fast enough to damage the reed (which at that time might have teeth of cane). But now he had before him a handle called the picker, from which two strings went to the left and right sides of the loom. Each of the strings was attached to a small block which lay in a slot running across the loom. If the picker was pulled so as to jerk the left-hand string, the block on that side leapt sharply along the slot and hit the shuttle, driving it to fly to the other end. The shuttle, which was loaded with a *pirn* of yarn, carried the weft through the shed in this way, and you can easily see that when it was propelled quickly, damage might often be done to the reed. Replacing reeds again and again would run away with the weaver's earnings, so the answer lay in buying the new steel reeds, even though they cost a lot to begin with.

Although the new reeds were so dear that they could really only be bought at first with help from the Board of Trustees or by several manufacturers clubbing together, there was no doubt that the flying shuttle was a very important improvement in the loom. For one thing, it meant that the weaver did not always have to change hands at his work: he could now work the picker with his right hand and beat up the weft with his left. Before, he had had to do this using his hands alternately. When he threw the shuttle across with his left hand, he beat up with his right, and then vice-versa. The new method was much quicker, much less complicated, and much less tiring.

And there was another advantage too. Before the invention of the flying shuttle, a weaver could only make what were called narrow cloths, usually three-quarters of a yard wide, because he could not comfortably throw the shuttle across the greater width. With the new invention, cloth could be woven the full width of the English yard.

By 1800 there were already a few broad-looms being used for the weaving of blankets, and over the years the quantity of broad cloths was gradually increased; but up till the 1830s at the least, the main advantage of the flying-shuttle was that it allowed for quicker weaving, and so for an increase in production. The width, of course, was also an important matter, because the Scots, who were accustomed to cloth which was not more than twenty-seven inches wide, could not hope to capture much of the English market until they began weaving it the full English yard in width.

8 Back to the Mill: Finishing

With the flying-shuttle, it would probably take a weaver about three days of steady work to finish the piece, but when it was cut from the loom and the weaver's part was done, it was certainly not ready to be made up into garments. It was still undyed: it sagged under its own weight; there were flaws in the weave here and there; and the surface was not covered with any of that short, slightly rough nap which a woollen cloth should have. So back it went to the mill again.

Now it was the turn of the dyer. Dyeing was considered a great skill, and its secrets were guarded carefully. In Galashiels, they did not usually dye the yarn but waited until the cloth was woven, and then dyed it 'in the piece'. The piece was soaked in a tub of hot dye-liquor until the colour had thoroughly sunk into it. In order to make sure that the colour was quite even, it was pushed down and stirred around in the dye with poles. You may feel that none of this sounds like very skilled work, but the real art in the dyer's trade lay in the use of dye-stuffs to produce fast colours in a variety of shades. This is far more difficult than it sounds, because wool reacts chemically with the dye-stuffs, and much skill is needed if the colour is to remain true throughout the entire piece and if it is not to fade patchily in strong light.

For some colours, vegetable dyes were used. These are some of the plants from which dyes were made in Scotland: alder bark and dock roots, to give black; dulse (a kind of seaweed), crotal (from lichens), blaeberries (known as bilberries in England), to give brown; dandelions, to give magenta; and bracken, to give yellow.

But many dyes were made from substances brought—often

at great expense—from foreign countries. Long before 1800 the big New Mills factory, which was set up with government help in the late seventeenth century, used these dyes: logwood (sometimes called Campeachy wood) to give blue; Barbados and Jamaica indigo, also to give blue; sumach, to give yellow; and cochineal, to give red. These were often ordered from wholesalers in the Low Countries who traded all over the world for them.

Other dye-stuffs which were sometimes used were saffron, which comes from the flowers of crocuses and gives a bright yellow colour; shellfish, whose juice yielded the brilliant purple known as 'Royal Tyrean'; cutch, which was a variety of acacia, and gave a brown colour; and copperas, known nowadays as green vitriol, which dyed black.

These raw materials were prepared in different ways to extract the dyes from them, and much knowledge and skill were needed to deal with substances which included wood, tree-bark, plant roots, stems, leaves and flowers, minerals and shellfish.

Whether these particular dyestuffs were used in Galashiels in 1800, we do not know, but it is likely that some of them were; if the dyers did not have such a wide selection to work with, at least they must have known how to mix those which they had to produce a variety of colours and shades.

Once the cloth had been soaked for long enough, it had to be dried before being finished. You may remember that one of the grants made by the Board of Trustees was for a drying house which was to be managed by the minister and the kirk-session. This house, which had been put up about 1787 and was ninety feet long, contained 'a stand of *tenters*'. To keep cloth firmly stretched as it dried, right-angled hooks were stuck through the edges and over a wooden framework—and these were, of course, known as tenterhooks. (Most of you will know what this means when we use it about somebody who is very anxious, and you can see how suitable it is.)

When the cloth was dry, it was time to find out all the flaws and put them right, where this could be done, before the piece was *milled*. There were a surprising number of things which   67 could go wrong, on the way from the bale of raw wool to the woven cloth. So it was hung across a bar beside a window and slowly pulled over it while a man looked at it carefully against the light. He could see where the weaver had not beaten up a line of weft, which was therefore lying slack; and where his foot had pressed the wrong treadle and he had passed the shuttle over and under the wrong threads. Then there were faults in the spinning of the yarn—thin parts which would not stand up to any wear, or thicknesses which showed up on the surface of the cloth. All of these, and many more, had to be marked with chalk, or in some other way, so that they could be repaired.

Now the cloth was flung face-down over a sloping table, and a worker would look for knots which the weaver had made when he had broken a warp or weft thread and had retied it. He became so skilled at this job that he could feel the knots as he passed his hands over the cloth quite as well as he could see them. His fingers became sensitive rather in the same way that those of a Braille reader do. He would draw the knots through to the back of the cloth so as to leave its face smooth. Threads which were too tight or too loose could be eased to the right tension from the selvedge. Where a thread was too tight, this probably meant breaking, easing it out and then mending the gap with yarn of the same kind.

In spite of the teazing and scouring which the wool had gone through before spinning, there were still some foreign bodies stuck in it. If these had been picked out while the wool was being carded, the sliver would have been badly weakened and the spun yarn would have been uneven. It was easier to remove them when they formed part of a close-packed woven surface which would not be badly damaged by having them picked out. With a spiked tool called a 'burling iron' fragments of straw, burs and prickles, which would have made the cloth unpleasantly scratchy to wear, were lifted out of it without damaging it. In some mills, too, there were machines which did this job by 1800.

You will remember that the piece, when it was cut from the loom, measured about seven yards, and that it was still rather thin and inclined to sag under its own weight. It could not leave the mill like that, especially since some of the knotting and mending which had been done on it was quite visible. It had to be milled or 'fulled', and this, of course, was the process which had been mechanised first of all. The waulk-mill, as you know, had used manpower in the form of human feet tramping the cloth as it lay in a trough of water mixed with *fuller's earth*. But then came the fulling-mills, which used water-power to drive heavy mallets which beat the cloth as it passed beneath them. These did a much better job, because the mallets could strike the cloth far more heavily than men's feet could. As they did so, the fibres of the wool became matted and felted into each other and the cloth gradually thickened. Meanwhile, of course, it shortened, because the beating which it was being given entangled the wool more closely, so that what was gained in thickness had to be lost from the length. In fact, a piece of cloth which went into the fulling-mill measuring seven yards would come out measuring about four and a half; and it came out scoured clean of all the stains which the oiled wool had picked up as it went through the carding engine, the jenny and the loom.

Once more, the piece was dried on the stand of tenters, and now it was getting close to being the finished article. But still it did not look quite like woollen cloth, because its surface was not yet covered with nap.

The work of 'raising' (making a pile on the cloth) was done by one of the strangest tools in the whole process from raw wool to cloth. This was 'Dipsacus fullorum', the wild teasel, which was a tall plant with big bullet-shaped heads about three inches high, covered all over with hooked scales. Some of you have probably seen it growing on waste ground. In the summer, the heads bear lots of small mauve flowers, and when these die the spikes slowly ripen in the autumn, turning downwards and becoming quite hard. Teasels had been used for raising cloth for a very long time, and the normal way of doing this was to cut off the pointed ends of the heads and mount them in rows in a flat frame with a handle which could be drawn, rather like a hairbrush, across the cloth. The down-turned hooks caught

Gig-mill for Teaselling

the wool-fibres and pulled them out into a nap. This was done with the cloth wet or dry, according to the effect which the manufacturer wanted to produce. It was very slow work, and by 1807 Richard Lees had got a £20 grant from the Board of Trustees for a *gig-mill* like the one you see here, to do the job by water-power, but hand-teaselling probably went on even after this in some of the mills.

Instead of the teasels being put in a small hand-frame, they were fitted all round the reel. While the cloth was carried round over the rollers, the reel holding the teasels rotated against it, and the surface of the cloth was automatically raised. This was such an improvement on hand-teaselling that one man could now do in ninety minutes what it had taken two men to do by hand in a whole day. For a while, teasels were even grown as a crop in gardens and fields in Selkirkshire, because so many were being used that they had to be brought in from outside; but the autumn sunlight in the Borders was not strong enough to harden the heads and make their spikes turn downwards to the correct angle, so this crop gradually died out in the county.

Before the cloth could receive its final pressing it had to be sheared, and you may remember that the Corporation grindstone was in regular use for sharpening shears. Perhaps it seems strange that the men should have raised the nap on the cloth only to cut it off again; but, for most purposes, it was too long and would soon have gathered into a series of little 'pills' on the surface of the material or would have looked untidily shaggy. The aim in shearing it was to leave enough on the face to blur the threads of the weave and to give the cloth a warm feel. This happened because air was trapped in the tangled pile and formed a barrier against the cold. Also, when there were different colours in the weave, the nap blended them together attractively on the face of the cloth.

The kind of shears which were used in the mills of Galashiels were unlike any which you might see nowadays. For one thing, they were very large, and both hands were needed to work them. Also, the blades did not cross each other like those of a pair of scissors: instead, when one blade lay flat on the cloth, the other came down to meet it at an angle and clipped the nap off as short as was necessary without pulling it. This was a very skilled job, and not one which an apprentice would be turned loose on! The shears were difficult to handle, and unless the nap was clipped evenly the whole appearance of the cloth might be ruined—and with it, the work of the carders, the spinners, the warpers and the weavers, not to mention the loss to the manufacturer. Now you can see why the shears had to be sharpened so often. They had to be really keen, and even when they were this was not a job which could be done quickly. But by 1811, Richard Lees had installed in his mill, not far from George Mercer's, a machine whose shears were driven by water. It was probably not unlike the one which you see on page 72, and which had not gone beyond the idea of giving water-power to a pair of shears of the old pattern. Even so, hand-shearing was the usual method of doing this work in most of the mills for some years yet.

Before very long, this clumsy arrangement was improved on,   71

Shearing-machine

and a guillotine was shearing the nap as the cloth passed round a roller; but even Richard Lees's shearing machine was so much more efficient than the old hand-tool that one man or boy could keep at least four pairs of water-driven shears going at once.

The work of raising the nap and shearing it was only done with woollens. If *worsteds* were being made, the nap was not raised, because worsted cloth had a smooth face on which the threads of the weave could be seen clearly.

The cloth was now ready to be pressed and folded before going to the Cloth Hall, or being sold by the travelling salesmen as they went on their rounds twice a year. When you think of the work that there is in ironing a sheet with a modern electric iron, you may wonder how, in the days of the old flat-iron, this job could be done neatly; but here, too, machines were being invented to do the work more quickly. Instead of trying to handle over four yards of cloth while smoothing it and keeping it uncreased after ironing, the men who were doing the finishing folded it, lengthwise first and then over on itself from end to end. Between each of the folds they put a metal plate, heated in an oven. When all this was weighted down from the top, the warmth and pressure combined to make the cloth smooth. The plates, of course, were not heated to a very high temperature because that would have damaged the face of the cloth.

When the plates were taken out, the cloth was folded neatly for the last time. After the scouring and the sorting, the carding and the spinning, the weaving and the finishing, it was ready for sale; and the manufacturer would do well if he sold it for more than 3s per yard.

9 Depression in the 1820s: The Coming of 'Tweeds'

Throughout the years from the first sale of woollen cloth in the Cloth Hall, Great Britain had been at war with France. George Mercer's sons grew up and worked alongside their father in Wilderhaugh Mill, and still the war against Napoleon dragged on. In the Borders, life went on against a background of rising prices; but now and then the war came closer. You will remember the night of 31 January 1804, when the beacon flared on the Eildons and the Volunteers marched off to defend Scotland against the French. Then there was the October day in 1805, when the bells rang out from every steeple to announce the victory at Trafalgar. Later on, the Border towns saw French soldiers at last! But they came as prisoners of war, not as invaders, and from 1811 to 1814 they passed the time as best they could in Selkirk and Melrose and other towns—though none actually seem to have been billetted in Galashiels. All of them were lodged in private houses, and they were not supposed to go more than a mile in any direction; but years later, one of them, Sous-Lieutenant Adelbert Doisy, wrote down his memories of imprisonment in Selkirk, which included fishing 'several miles down the Tweed' and dining with the Sheriff, Mr Scott, at Abbotsford, three miles away. For the most part, the prisoners seemed to get on well in the Borders, but they were glad when at last, in 1814, peace was made between France and her enemies, and they were sent home. Sous-Lieutenant Doisy wrote that: 'We had all passed the night in the public gardens, singing and amusing ourselves, so that we were ready in good time and were going to start out when an unexpected and odd sight met our eyes. Vehicles of all kinds came from all the streets towards the centre of the town—carriages, *tilburys*, wagons, even saddle-horses—all sent by the people living in the neighbourhood to take us free of charge to Kelso, halfway to Berwick.'

After Waterloo, in 1815, people may have hoped that life would become easier again, but in some ways things became worse, not better. Factories which had been working flat-out during the war started paying men off because the demand for their goods had slackened; farm-hands were being turned off because farmers, who had ploughed every foot of land on which they could grow wheat, were now letting some of it go back to fallow and needed fewer labourers on their farms; soldiers were coming back from the war to find that they could get no work. On top of this, wages (which had been high during the war) were falling, while the price of bread remained high; and poor-relief rates were so small that they did little to save thousands of families from distress. In some industrial towns in England, there was rioting and machine-breaking by men who feared that it was the machines which were putting them out of work. In Galashiels, there was a good deal of unrest, but no serious trouble between masters and men. There were noisy crowds, shouting for, 'Nae mair *braid* looms', but no factory-burning.

In 1819 the Manufacturers' Corporation sent a petition to Parliament, protesting against the Government's plan to put a tax on foreign wool coming into the country. They said that the tax would only help land-owners who raised sheep and that it would make the foreign wool, which they needed to blend with the coarser British wool, very dear. They also warned the Government of the dangers which came from having large numbers of men out of work.

These were hard years for the weavers who were idle or on short time. They spent long hours, hanging round their own doors and watching to see whether anybody would come down from the mill with some warp to be woven. Their neighbours might be lucky one day: they might have the luck the next. But when the days passed without work to do, the men became restless because it was hard to keep their self- 75 respect when they could not provide for their families. The broth got thinner because there was less to put in it, and the children's faces grew pinched with hunger, but the weavers could do nothing except hope for better times and exist on the charity of their neighbours after their own savings were gone. Small wonder that some of them were sometimes tempted to throw what little they had away on a dram, so as to forget their troubles, even for a short while!

The slackness in the woollen trade was not due simply to the effects of the war. For a long time, Galashiels had mainly been making one kind of cloth, the 'Galashiels Greys', which were twenty-seven inches wide. This had been suitable enough when most of the town's trade was local, but a change in fashion had followed the hard years after 1815—just as fashions changed sharply at the end of clothes-rationing in the early 1950s. Traditional colours—grey, blue and drab—were out of fashion, and Galashiels had to make new kinds of cloth or else lose its customers. So the weavers tried out 'twists', which were yarns of different colours twisted together and woven that way. These gave interesting new effects. Slowly, trade began to improve a little, but times were still hard and, as late as 1829, twenty manufacturers went out of business in one year.

Towards the end of the 1820s came the demand for checks. As usual, a few bold spirits led the fashion, appearing in public in trousers woven in the black and white checks of the shepherd tartan from which the shepherd mauds had been made. For once, it was not London which set the fashion, but as soon as a few Scotsmen (particularly when they were as famous as Sir Walter Scott) had been seen wearing the stylish new checked trousers, London seized on the idea and began to demand pieces forty yards in length. And once the idea of checks had been accepted, people began to ask for checks of other colours. This was difficult for the manufacturers, because they were still dyeing cloth 'in the piece' for the most part, but they soon hit on the idea of producing black and brown checks by soaking a black and white piece in brown dye, which would be taken up by the white checks. Not long after this, they were making black and green, as well as black and blue, checks in the same way. But there were limits to what they could do by piece-dyeing, and in any case the new cloths were only produced in small quantities by the cautious weavers, because they did not expect the fashion to last and did not want to be left with yards of cloth unsold.

By the mid-1830s the London trade was growing steadily, and the weavers were trying out checks of different sizes, and also what were known as 'broken checks'. These gave an all-over check look, but close to, the squares were seen to be broken in outline, and this made a more interesting effect. All the same, the new fancy cloths were still only a small part of what was made in Galashiels. The looms could never have been kept going all the year round on weaving fancy cloths—especially when the whole output of this kind for Scotland was worth £3000 in 1832. Still, the woollen trade in Galashiels was growing, as you will see if you look at the table below:

1792	*1833*
Number of looms: about 43	Number of looms: about 130
Number of weavers: about 50	Number of weavers: about 100
Amount of wool used per year: about 2916 stones	Amount of wool used per year: about 21500 stones
Made into: narrow cloths, blankets, some flannels, and worsteds	About half made into flannels, blankets, shawls, plaids and stockings.
	The rest into narrow cloths mostly, but some into broad cloths including fancy ones.

If you had asked one of the manufacturers in the 1830s how much tweed his looms were turning out each year, he would have stared at you—because 'tweed' to a Scotsman at that time meant only one thing: the River Tweed. But if you had asked him to tell you what 'tweels' were, that would have been quite another story. For all the cloths which were being turned out in Galashiels at this time—whether they were narrow or broad, heavy or light in weight, self-coloured or twisted or checked—were called tweels by Scotsmen (and twills by Englishmen). Tweels were a cloth which was woven so that each thread crossed over two or under two others, while the

77

weave appeared to move upwards to the right or the left like this:

Common Twill Weave

In 1840, a Hawick firm sent the invoice for a parcel of tweel to a London merchant, John Locke, and, whether it was written carelessly in Hawick or read hastily in London, what had been common tweel in a checked pattern became 'tweed', the trade-name for a cloth which soon seemed as Scottish as tartan or haggis!

It would not be right to say that the Border woollen trade was made by the invention of tweed, because it has had its ups and downs ever since 1840; but once the finer wools from Germany and elsewhere were brought in to make a cloth with a softer feel, the skills of the Border spinners and weavers, the piecers and warpers, the dyers and finishers, were able to produce the cloth for which the Borders have become famous: the warm, slightly rough cloth whose endless variety of colours is drawn from the hills, the stones and the whins, heather and bracken of the Borders.

In Galashiels, tweed is still made in the same narrow valley which Dorothy Wordsworth saw when she passed through the Borders in 1803 and gave a disapproving glance at the village with its 'manufactory' and its 'townish bustle'.

10 *Marketing*

By now, you will have realised that the Border woollen trade depended a lot on the roads. Shepherds had to drive sheep from one farm to another, or to one of the stock-markets, and fleeces had to be carried from the farms to the wool-markets and to the mills. As the trade increased and manufacturers became interested in new inventions, machines had to be brought from England to be set up in the mills. Finished goods of course had to be taken to the customers, and these were not just local any longer, but were in Edinburgh, Glasgow and even London.

How was this done? Nowadays, we can rely on the telephone or on a rapid postal system to pass on orders from customer to supplier, and on good roads and railway lines to transport the goods from the mills to the markets. But what were communications like in Selkirkshire when Dr Douglas was parish minister and when George Mercer was putting new machines into Wilderhaugh Mill?

It was not until 1848 that the railway came to Galashiels, so until then, everything that came into or went out of the village or the county had to go by road—and you may remember that, almost as late as 1800, it was not unknown for carters to use the bed of Gala Water rather than the highway from Edinburgh.

Still, there were differences, even among the roads of that time. The main highway through the county was the Edinburgh to Carlisle road (now the A7). This passed to the west of Galashiels instead of running through it, as it does today, and went on to Selkirk and Hawick. A branch from it crossed Gala Water north of the village and went on to Melrose. Since both these roads, which were kept in fairly good repair, by-passed Galashiels, it was not very well placed for keeping in touch even with the places nearest to it.

Apart from these two main roads, running roughly north and south, there were two others running more or less east and west. These were built from Selkirk up Ettrick and Yarrow, with the idea of linking Selkirk and Moffat, in Dumfriesshire. If this could be done, it would be far easier to travel across the country. But although these roads were said to be 'formed', they were certainly not fully made up, and in wet weather, according to a report of 1794, were 'almost impassable'. It was along one of these roads that Alexander Laidlaw had to drive his flocks to market.

Worse still were the side-roads. They were 'in a state of nature', i.e. they had not been made at all. They were those bits of the open country which happened to have been used so much by men and animals that they became roads, but they were full of great ruts and deep pot-holes and were really dangerous.

One way of improving roads at this time was by making them into *turnpikes*. By charging people for using a length of road, the turnpike company could make money to pay for repairing it. When a turnpike trust was to be set up in Selkirk-shire, rules were made for using the road, and these give us some idea of what highways were like around 1800. For instance, mileposts had to be put up, and there were to be signposts at cross-roads to show where the side-lanes led to. Then there were to be penalties for driving ploughs or harrows on the roads, or for hauling timber or stone on them except in a wheeled cart. Holes were not to be dug in the roads, and if a farmer wanted to get rid of an old horse which had at last died, one place where he must not leave its carcase was the middle of the turnpike! And last of all, everybody had to drive on the left side of the road.

All this sounds as though people had had a rather light-hearted attitude to roads and their upkeep, using them as rubbish-dumps or as sandpits, according to the whim of the moment, or even as burial-grounds for worn-out horses. It is

A country scene

easy to see why, when there were no milestones and few sign-posts, a Scottish mile (which was certainly longer than an English one) was thought of by English visitors as a vague distance which, after a very long time, might lead them to their destination—or might not!

As well as these, there were the roads along which herds of cattle were driven from central Scotland down over the Border to be fattened for the English markets. The 'drove-roads' were not made up at all; in fact, they were simply the tracks beaten out across hills, through valleys and over rivers by the hooves of the slow-moving cattle for year after year. And they might sometimes be the quickest way of crossing from one river-valley to another. Two of these drove-roads crossed from the Tweed valley over the watershed and down into Yarrow not far from the eastern end of St Mary's Loch. Then they climbed up again over the next range of hills and crossed a high plateau of boggy, windswept moorland before they dropped down to meet in Ettrick. From there, they went south as one track for some miles and then divided again, one fork branching off

F

down towards Gretna and Carlisle, and the other crossing some of the loneliest Border lands to the source of the Northumberland Tyne.

This was certainly one way of avoiding the mud, the dust and the potholes of the main roads, but a man who used the drove-roads did so at his own risk, for he could expect no help from passers-by if he met thieves. There were no passers-by over those desolate moorlands.

Almost more of a hindrance to good communications was the lack of bridges over the three main rivers. In 1800 a shepherd in Ettrick or Yarrow might have to drive his flock for miles downstream before he could cross. It was true that there were fords here and there, but these could be treacherous in a country where an hour's rain could turn a gentle, shallow stretch of water into an angry, swirling torrent. So bridges over both rivers were badly needed, but there was an even greater need of a bridge over the Tweed near to where Gala Water joined it. Anybody who wished to go from Galashiels to Selkirk had to cross the Tweed by the ferry at this point, which was slow and inconvenient, or else go several miles out of his way to the main Edinburgh-Carlisle road. The ferry could even be dangerous, and on one occasion lives had been lost when it turned turtle.

With roads like these, it was little wonder that almost all of the carrier-work of the area had been done by pack-horses, up to at least 1750. But by 1800 there were sixty-four carts in the parish of Galashiels, and over ninety horses used for carting: everything that came into the village or went out from it was carried in carts, whether it was coal or grain, wool or manure. (So now you can see why three blacksmiths were needed in the village.)

Regular carrier-services grew up as time went by, and a merchant or a manufacturer would pay a carrier to take goods to Selkirk or Melrose, to Edinburgh or even to Newcastle-on-Tyne, just as we can now pay British Road Services to carry heavy parcels for us in trucks. You can see that this was a very slow way of moving goods, since the carts had often to travel up and down hills and could do so only at the walking-pace of a single horse or a pair. Yet, as late as 1840, the Manufacturers' Corporation made an agreement with a carrier's company to take finished woollen goods to Edinburgh and bring back raw materials and supplies twice a week by cart.

Where we use the telephone to make business arrangements, manufacturers used the post, slow though it was. Yet Galashiels had no post-office until the 1820s. Until then, letters from the south were sent by coach to Melrose or Selkirk or Stagehall, which was seven miles north of Galashiels on the Edinburgh road. A messenger would ride or walk there regularly with outgoing letters which he handed over and would come back to Galashiels with the incoming mail. Not only was this a slow service, but it was also quite a dear one. The days of the penny post had not arrived yet, and a letter from Galashiels to Melrose cost 4d, as it does today, while postage to London cost 7d, and a letter to America 2s 5d. Correspondence must have been cut down to what was absolutely necessary, and certainly every letter was made to carry the maximum of writing, so as to be worth the heavy cost. Sometimes, when a sheet had been filled from side to side, it was turned round and written on from end to end.

Street Auctioner

Manufacturers also kept in direct touch with their customers by making trips at least twice a year through the areas where they sold their goods. Riding one horse and leading a pack-animal laden with samples of cloth, they would visit merchants and tailors in towns and villages as they went. Sometimes they carried with them a stick on which were wound the different colours of yarn in which the cloths could be woven. In other words, they acted as their own sales representatives, just as the pedlar in the picture on page 83 is acting like a door-to-door salesman of today.

Some of them might have a purely local trade, in Selkirkshire and Berwickshire, for example, but others would go further afield, like the manufacturer whose ledger shows that, between 1805 and 1818, he dealt with customers in Midlothian, Fife, Forfar, Kincardineshire, Banff, Elgin, Perth and Stirling. They would carry wherever they went the news of the patterns which were 'in' and the colours which were fashionable, and there would be much leisurely discussion over the counter before bargains were struck.

At the same time, manufacturers collected their debts from their customers—if they could. The usual way of doing business in the woollen trade was rather like the slogan which you sometimes see in shops today, 'Buy now—pay later'. The manufacturer sold cloth to his customers in, say, April, and they did not have to pay for it until October. When he made his round in October, he hoped to collect the money which was owed to him, because he had already had to pay for the raw wool, not to speak of the wages of spinners, weavers and others, so as to make the cloth. And these early manufacturers were not rich men: far from it! They were weavers themselves, just like their men, but they had the ability and energy to strike out and build up their businesses, even if this meant taking risks. So they were willing to go to England and buy new machinery there in the hope of increasing production; and they would build new mills—and re-build them when they went on fire, as happened twice at Wilderhaugh—even when they had to borrow the money to do so. In the same way, they would

sell cloth 'on long credit' to their customers, although they had little money behind them. They were enterprising men, but many of them must have sighed with relief as they rode home with their pockets heavy with money at the end of a trip.

Although we know that Galashiels woollens were sold widely in Scotland, we cannot be quite sure whether they were exported or not. But we do know that woollens from Scotland were sold outside the country. From the whole of Great Britain, woollens were sent to twenty-five countries, from Asia in the east to North America in the west, and they were sold from Norway to Africa. The Customs returns show us this: they also tell us the different kinds of woollen goods which were exported, as well as their value. Fine cloths and duffles, baizes and carpets, blankets and stockings all went overseas, and in one year, 1817, they earned almost £8 million.

It seems quite likely that some of these came from Galashiels. From Leith, for example, woollens were shipped to the Baltic countries and north Germany, as well as being carried by coast-wise ships to London for the market there. And from Glasgow, there was a steady export trade to America and the West Indies. There were firms in Glasgow which handled

The Port of Leith

these exports, and we know that Galashiels manufacturers dealt with some of these firms. This is why it seems likely that some of the cloth woven in dark cottage-kitchens in Galashiels found its way to America, and some may even have reached the steamy heat of the Plantations. It was natural that Scottish 85 emigrants to America should want to buy tartan cloths, which would remind them of home, and they were probably glad of the heavy duffles. Possibly it was the superfine cloths which were bought in the West Indies, since these would be the lightest in weight.

When we remember all the difficulties of bad roads, slow postal services, transport by pack-horse, cart or sailing-ship, lack of money and the habit of giving long credit to customers, it is amazing that men like George Mercer, James Sanderson and Richard Lees were willing to take on the worry of making and marketing woollen-cloth, not only in Scotland, but in England and even, perhaps, across the Atlantic.

But, though they were buying wool from Germany, Spain and even Van Diemen's Land and selling their products far and wide, the manufacturers remained close to their workers. In Galashiels there was little of the unrest which was common elsewhere: you remember that, where Nottingham had machine-breaking, Galashiels had a rowdy meeting which went no further than cries of, 'Nae mair braid looms!' And when, in 1849, the first strike in the Galashiels woollen trade at last happened over a pay dispute, the manufacturers themselves gave the weavers introductions to employers in other woollen towns so that they could check the figures on which the mill-owners based their offer!

Where does the Information come from?

Most of the things that you have been reading about in this book happened between 1790 and 1825, and, since all the people in the story have been dead for a very long time, you might ask how we know about them and their lives?

There are quite a lot of ways of finding out, but one of the main ones is by reading things which were written at that time: 'things', you notice, not 'books'. Of course, we do read books, but we also read letters, and we look at accounts, and leases drawn up by lawyers in their own kind of English, and Acts of Parliament, and customs returns, and other things of that sort. These things are not usually collected tidily for us in one place. We have to go and look for them— and this means going to libraries, and writing to people who might have bundles of old papers and asking them to let us see them.

Then, we can look at old maps and pictures. We can compare maps of about 1800 with presentday ones, and we can often, from a picture, get a far clearer idea of how people dressed, or what their houses were like, than from a lot of written description. And then, if a picture of a man or woman in 1800 corresponds with a description about the same time, we can be fairly sure that we are getting at the truth.

By visiting museums, too, we can sometimes see the very kind of thing which we have been reading about in books: a shuttle perhaps, or a reed.

In writing this story, several books written between 1790 and 1802 about the farming and industry of Selkirkshire have been used, and some papers belonging to the Manufacturers' Corporation of Galashiels have shown how the Corporation spent its income each year, and who became apprenticed to the trade, and who got fined for not turning up to meetings. A book written by one of the great Ettrick landowners, and published in 1822, gave a lot of information about hill-farming at that time, and a huge encyclopaedia, which came out in 1810, supplied a great deal of detail about woollen manufacture. The illustrations of machines were mostly found there, too.

In one library, whole volumes of maps could be consulted, some of them very like ordinary maps in a school atlas, some large-scale town maps, and even some road-maps in strips—like the kind of route-map which motoring organizations hand out if you want to know the best way from Glasgow to Birmingham, for example.

Then, a visit to a modern mill brought to life much of the reading. Although all sorts of new machines had been developed, and although far more interesting patterns and colours could be produced than the mills could turn out in 1800, it was still possible to see that processes like carding and spinning and weaving had not changed completely since then.

And last of all, a journey up Ettrick and Yarrow, where our story began, showed that it is still—on a weekday, at least—lonely there. There are not many more people now than there were in 1798, when Dr Douglas wrote about Selkirkshire, and the sheep feel so safe that they scamper down the hillsides and across the fine new road which runs past St Mary's Loch towards Moffat right in front of passing cars. And it is still on sheep and their wool that the prosperity of Galashiels largely depends.

All this has been the raw material of our story, and what we have made out of it is just one of the ways in which it could have been used.

Things to do

1. Make your own map of the Borders and mark on it the places where there were looms at work near the end of the eighteenth century.

   See whether your public library has a map of your own area at about 1800 and copy its main outlines. If you live in a city, you will probably find that a town map of 1800 gives you a surprise. For a country area you may not be able to get a map of 1800, but get the earliest one that you can.

2. In Selkirkshire, the main occupations were mostly to do with sheep and wool. Try to find out whether there was one outstanding kind of occupation in your area around 1800; for example, coal-mining, dairy-farming or ship-building. Now make a list of people's trades and occupations in your area today. (This can just be a rough list done from memory.) Make a note of the main changes in occupations since 1800.

3. If there have been big changes, can you find out any reason why they have happened?

4. You have seen how the lie of the hills and the course of the rivers in Selkirkshire helped to shut it off from the north and south. Do you live in an area where hills and river-valleys make it difficult to keep in touch with other parts of the country? Look at the map of your area from around 1800 and see where the roads led to and whether they had to climb hills or cross rivers to reach market-towns or ports.

5. Find out how houses were built in your area in 1800. What materials were used? What was used for roofing them? How many storeys did they mostly have? If there are any labourers' cottages of that time still standing, find out their measurements and draw them. Compare these with houses in other parts of the country by finding books about this in your library.

6. See if your nearest museum has any cottage furniture and household goods dating from about 1800. How do they differ from the furnishings of the cottages in Selkirkshire?

7. Make out a shopping list of the things which your family would buy at these shops: grocer, butcher, baker, fishmonger and greengrocer. Compare your list with the kind of food which people ate in Selkirkshire in 1800. How much of your list consists of things which they ate too? How much of your list consists of (a), tinned and (b), imported foods which they could not have eaten? In what ways do you think your diet is better than theirs? What would you miss most if you had to live on their diet?

8. Have you any special games which are played at different times of the year in your area, like the Fastern's E'en handball game in Galashiels? Describe them.

9. How does the school in Galashiels differ from yours? If there is a school in your area which has been going for a long time, its log-book may be in the public library, or there may be a history of it there. Compare what the pupils learned there in 1800 with the work done at the Galashiels school, and with the subjects which you learn now.

10. How is your town or your area governed? Who decides what will be done to improve it? What services are there in it (e.g. buses, swimming baths)? Compare this with the picture which you have got of Galashiels in 1800, remembering that it was a place of less than 1000 people. What do you think was the most serious way in which their standards fell below ours?

11. What part does the Church play in people's lives where you live? Make a note of the kind of works which the Kirk or its minister did in Galashiels. Some of these have now been taken over by other people; find out who does them today.

12. In 1800, people's health suffered because their surroundings were dirty, or because they worked too long hours or could not afford enough good food. Who looks after public health now, and who settles hours of work and rates of pay?

Selkirkshire people at work

13. Make a list of all the things that happened to wool before it became cloth, and write down in a sentence or two what each process was meant to do. Perhaps you could divide the class into groups for this, so that half of it did the processes as far as spinning and the other half did the rest.

14. Different parts of woollen manufacture were mechanised at different times in Galashiels. See if you can work out how the following processes were done (a), in 1780 and (b), in 1800: carding, spinning, weaving, milling, raising and shearing.

15. Which parts of the work were done at home and which were done by water-power in the mill, in 1800?

16. How was a weaver's life in 1800 different from the life of a factory worker now?

17. In some parts of the country there are still water-wheels working. If there is a local history society in your area, they may be able to tell you of any water-driven mills. Try to visit one and see how it works and how the power is passed on to the mill-machinery. Then you can judge better how the use of water-power changed the woollen industry.

18. If you live in a place where woollens are manufactured, try to get taken over a woollen-mill and compare the processes that you see there with those in the Galashiels mills about 1800.

19. You may be lucky enough to have in your area a firm which makes hand-woven woollens. If so, try to see a hand-loom at work, and watch all the weaver's movements, remembering that they will be very like those of a weaver in 1800. If you have no firm like this near you, your local museum may have working models of hand-looms.

20. In your school's craft department, you may be able to weave a strip of woollen-cloth on a small loom. This would give you a clearer idea about weaving than you will get just from reading about it.

21. You might carry this a bit further by felting your strip, or part of it. This can be done by putting it in hot water for a while and then rubbing it hard. (You might do this at home, since it will take some time, and bring the felted strip to school.) You can then see the effect of felting by comparing it with unfelted cloth.

22. What difference do you notice between the day-to-day life of the mother of a family in 1800 and of mothers today?

23. If you live in the country, try to find out how the land around your home was farmed in 1800; and if you live in a town with one important industry, find out all that you can about how it was carried on in 1800.

Drawings, paintings, stories, etc.

24. Paint a picture of the kitchen of a labourer's cottage in 1800, using both the written description and the illustration.

25. Write the story of a shepherd who goes out in a snowstorm to save his flocks.

26. Describe a day's journey in about 1800 to one of the Galashiels markets, from the point of view of a shepherd with some sheep to sell. What price would you try to get for your lambs and what would you tell your family about Galashiels when you got home?

27. Write a scene about one of the big fairs, with parts for all the people who might be there, and act it in your classroom.

28. Work with the rest of the class to draw or paint a series of pictures illustrating the idea, 'Wool: from the Sheep's back to cloth'. The pictures could go, in the form of a frieze, along one wall, and perhaps those who cannot draw could write a sentence to explain each picture.

29. Write a conversation between a young weaver and an old one in which each sticks up for the woollen industry as he has known it. Speak it to the class.

30. Make a map for the classroom wall, showing the markets to which Scottish woollens were sent.
31. Imagine yourself to be an apprentice in a Galashiels mill in 1800 and write the story of your first day at work.

The Weavers' Letter to Dr Douglas (p.17)
Sir,

We suppose that you have heard the repeated complaints of our cloths being so narrow which obliged us to adapt the Leeds plan in erecting fly shuttles and indeed many of us is standing indebted to the tradesman for the expense owing to our want of stock . . . The reed makers tell us nothing but steel reeds will stand which is altogether out of our power to purchase and we are persuaded that if the matter was represented to the Honourable Board of Trustees by any kind person they could lend their aid to purchase such a necessary thing, for unless we be helped we will be reduced to our old way . . .

Glossary

accoutrements, soldier's equipment.

ambry, a wooden cupboard.

bailie, magistrate in a town, corresponding to an alderman in England.

baron-bailie, magistrate in a barony, appointed by the laird.

barony, in Scotland, an estate granted to a person by the king.

braid, broad.

burgh of barony, a burgh which has been granted to a person and his descendants as their own estate.

burs, fruits of certain plants, which cling to the fleece of sheep by tiny hooks. Goose-grass has fruits like these.

byre, a cow-house.

cantle, the crown of the head.

card, a flat board, fitted with teeth, which was drawn over a bunch of wool to straighten out the fibres. To card is to do this job.

cast-ewe, a female sheep, four to six years old, of no further use for breeding. Sometimes known as a 'crock'.

caulm, small cords with loops or eyes in them, through which warp-threads were passed in the loom. Also known as heddles or healds in some parts of the country.

chincough, whooping-cough.

clarty, dirty, muddy.

cleading, clothing.

cleuch, a narrow and often steep valley in hill-country. Much the same as a 'combe' in England.

close-bed, a bed with doors which could be closed to shut out light.

convivial, cheerful, enjoyable.

crack, a conversation, a chat.

darg, the tenant's duty of doing a day's work for his landlord as a condition of his tenancy.

doffer, a cylinder which stripped off the wool from the carding engine. The person who did this job.

dominie, a schoolmaster: from the Latin word *dominus,* a master.

drafting, drawing out: so draft is the length to which a spinner drew out the carded sliver to make it into yarn.

dram, a drink, usually of spirits.

dyke, a wall: often built, in Scotland, of stones fitted together without mortar.

Egyptians, gypsies.

ewe-hog, the name given to a young ewe from her first Martinmas smearing until her first clipping in the following July, i.e. from 5-15 months old.

Fastern's E'en, Shrove Tuesday, i.e. the day before the beginning of the Lenten fast on Ash Wednesday.

fuller's earth, a kind of earth used by fullers in thickening and cleaning cloth.

gauger, another name for the exciseman. A very unpopular person who not only collected duties for the government but also looked for and destroyed 'illicit stills', i.e. stills in which people were making whisky without having a licence to do so.

gig-mill, a mill for raising nap on cloth by the use of teasels.

gimmer, the name given to a ewe from her first clipping until her second one, i.e. from about 15-27 months old.

great-ewe, a ewe which was carrying a lamb.

greetin', weeping.

halberd, a weapon with a head which had both a sharp blade and a stabbing point, set on a six-foot handle.

halflins, half-way.

haugh, land in the bottom of a valley, often on either side of a river.

ilka, each.

imprimis, in the first place, firstly.

indenture, a contract made between a master and an apprentice.

jenny, a machine by means of which a number of threads could be spun at the same time.

kain, the tenant's duty of providing his landlord with a certain number of tame fowls each year.

Kilmarnock bonnet, the flat cap worn by some of the men in the pictures.

Kirk Session, the body of elders who, together with the minister, were responsible for running the life of the parish.

laird, a landowner. In a burgh of barony the laird held his land directly from the Crown.

maud, a plaid in the shepherd check worn in the Border country.

midden, a manure-heap.

milled, cloth was beaten with heavy wooden hammers so as to make it felt or thicken-up.

mill-lade, a channel for leading water to a mill-wheel.

monopoly, the right given to one person or one firm to make or sell a particular kind of goods in one place.

mort, the skin of a lamb or sheep which has died by accident or from disease.

Mountain Dew, a name for whisky; sometimes used for whisky made in an illicit still (see *gauger*).

mule, a machine for spinning several threads at once, using water-power.

pattens, wooden overshoes consisting of a sole mounted on an iron ring. These raised the wearer an inch or two out of the mud of the street.

pirn, a bobbin of yarn used in a shuttle by the weaver.

policies, the enclosed park surrounding a country house.

randy, disorderly.

Redundant, used nowadays in industry to mean workers who lose their jobs because the firm is already employing too many men for the work which it is doing.

reed, a comb-shaped frame which was used to beat each new line of weft against the last one.

revolutions, turns.

scribbler, a machine used in carding wool.

Seal of Cause, a legal document by which a craft society was recognized as a corporation in a burgh.

shalloons, materials used for linings.

shuttle, a container holding a pirn or bobbin. It is passed from side to side of the loom and carries the weft-thread over and under the warp.

slubber, a worker who operated a slubbing billy.

sluice-gate, a barrier across a water-channel, which can be raised or lowered to control the flow of water.

souter, a shoe-maker.

staple, the length and fineness of the fibre in a particular type of wool.

tack, a leasehold tenancy agreement.

tawse, the leather strap used for punishing pupils in Scottish schools.

teazing willie, see under 'willy'. Teazing was the process of loosening out the wool to get rid of the dirt.

tenters, wooden frames over which cloth was stretched to dry.

thrums, the ends of the warp-threads which remained attached to the loom when the piece was cut out.

tilbury, an open, two-wheeled carriage.

tolbooth, a name given either to the town hall or to the town jail.

tup, the name given to a male sheep from the time of first clipping onwards, i.e. from about 15 months old.

turnpike, a road on which barriers were placed to hold up traffic until a toll had been paid. The money raised at the toll-gates was used for the upkeep of the stretch of road.

warp, threads running from end to end of a piece of cloth.

waulk-mill, originally, a mill consisting of a trough in which people simply walked up and down, tramping on the finished cloth as it lay in water, so as to 'full' or felt it.

weft, threads running across a piece of cloth.

whin, gorse or furze.

willy or willie, came from the word 'willow'. At one time the wool was beaten with willow branches to knock the dust out of it and loosen it out for carding.

winna, won't.

worsted, a woollen cloth with a smooth face.
wright, a craftsman, particularly a joiner.